P9-DFU-755

# Our Mickey

## CHERISHED MEMORIES OF AN AMERICAN ICON

# Our Mickey

## CHERISHED MEMORIES OF AN AMERICAN ICON

**Bill Liederman and Maury Allen**

TRIUMPH
BOOKS
CHICAGO

Copyright © 2004 by Bill Liederman and Maury Allen

No part of this publication may be reproduced, stored in a retrieval system, or transmitted, in any form by any means, electronic, mechanical, photocopying, or otherwise, without the prior written permission of the publisher, Triumph Books, 601 S. LaSalle St., Suite 500, Chicago, Illinois 60605.

Library of Congress Cataloging-in-Publication Data

Liederman, Bill, 1952–

    Our Mickey : cherished memories of an American icon / Bill Liederman and Maury Allen.

    p. cm.

    Includes index.

    ISBN 1-57243-598-4

    1. Mantle, Mickey, 1931—Anecdotes. 2. Mantle, Mickey, 1931—Friends and associates. 3. Baseball players—United States—Anecdotes. I. Allen, Maury, 1932– II. Title.

    GV865.M33L54 2004

    796.357'092—dc22

    [B]

2003063400

This book is available in quantity at special discounts for your group or organization. For further information, contact:

Triumph Books

601 South LaSalle Street

Suite 500

Chicago, Illinois 60605

(312) 939-3330

Fax (312) 663-3557

Printed in U.S.A.

ISBN 1-57243-598-4

Design by Eileen Wagner, Wagner/Donovan Design

To my wife, Tracy, and with special thanks to Maury and Janet Allen. Their encouragement made this book possible. And to my daughter Chloe, for her brilliant editing.

—B.L.

---

To Amanda, Matthew, and Ben

—M.A.

*With love, happiness, and joy*

# Contents

Mickey Mantle was a great teammate of mine. He hit a lot of home runs for the Yankees. He seemed to hit plenty of them when it mattered most, late in the game or in the World Series. I think he had 18 in the Series. I only hit 12. But I played in a lot more World Series games than Mickey and cashed a lot more Series checks.

He had a lot of pressure on him when he first came up in 1951. Joe DiMaggio was playing center field for the Yankees then. He was the best there was. So Mickey played right field, and when he began striking out a lot, Casey Stengel sent him down to Kansas City.

He came back later that year and took over center field the next season. In a few more years he was about the best in the game with that Triple Crown in 1956. Like Casey used to say, "You could look it up." He led the league in home runs with 52, won the batting title, and led the league in RBIs.

We just seemed to win every year. That's what made playing for the Yankees so much fun.

In 1961 Mickey and Roger Maris put on quite a show. Roger hit 61 to break the Babe Ruth mark, and Mickey hit 54. He got hurt at the end of the year, and if he hadn't, they both would have passed the Babe I think.

I hit 22 homers that year. John Blanchard hit 21, and so did Ellie Howard. We used to kid Mickey and Roger that the Yankees catchers (combined) hit more than either of them.

I managed Mickey in 1964 but he got hurt a lot. He played good when he could.

I know his last couple of years were painful for him with the injuries and all, but Mickey always gave it his best shot.

We saw a lot of each other, after we both quit, at banquets and golf tournaments and all those baseball events. Mickey was always fun to be around.

I saw him at the end when he was real sick. He was as brave about that as he had been facing the toughest pitcher in the game in the toughest spot.

This book has a lot of people telling their favorite stories about Mickey. I think you will get a kick out of reading it. It brings back a lot of great memories.

You know what? I still miss him, and I always will.

—Yogi Berra

# Mickey Remembered

Mickey Mantle.

Maybe it was just that name. Maybe it was the way he walked to the plate or jogged, head down, around the bases after crushing a baseball into the far-right-field stands at Yankee Stadium or over the Green Monster at Fenway Park or into the palm trees in some Florida training camp.

Maybe it was that short blond hair, those deep blue eyes, that incredible athletic body, that flat stomach, those thick shoulders and muscular neck.

It could simply be that classic No. 7 in the center of his pinstriped New York Yankees uniform that fans studied for 18 glorious seasons from the dashing days of 1951 until the twilight moments of 1968.

"He was the first blond I ever fell in love with," said former Yankees batboy Thad Mumford, who grew up to become an Emmy-winning television writer on *M\*A\*S\*H* and *Maude*. "The second one was Marilyn Monroe."

Mantle joined the Yankees out of his hometown of Commerce, Oklahoma, the son of a zinc miner father and a strong, dedicated, homemaker mother. His father, Elvin "Mutt" Mantle, died before his 40th birthday, and his mother, Lovell, lived into her nineties with care and comfort from her famous son.

Mickey and Merlyn Mantle had four strong and handsome sons, but only two, David and Danny, survive as legacies of the glorious baseball years, the difficulties of separation, and the enormous bonding of the final summers.

It was not just the 536 home runs, some as distant as a new time zone, or the 18 World Series homers in 12 different seasons, or the three MVP titles, or the brilliant catches, or even the calm leadership he provided.

There was something so unique, so special, so incredible about the style of Mickey Mantle, the way he played, the way he lived, the way he talked, the way he laughed. Oh, that laugh, up from the gut and out of the mouth, roaring into a clubhouse, a banquet room, a television studio, a family living room, his face bursting with childlike glee.

In the 1961 season he electrified the country with his teammate and pal, Roger Maris, in the most thrilling, most dramatic, most emotional home-run race in the history of the game.

Mickey was the favorite, 10 years a Yankee, as he blasted home runs from both sides of the plate, reaching ever faster for the record set 34 years earlier by Babe Ruth. Maris was the new guy in town, only a second-year Yankee, and some of the Yankees players and lots of the fans saw his challenge as an invasion.

Mickey saw it only as pure, energizing, fundamental competition. That's what a home-run race was all about. Mickey and Roger were friends, pulling together for another Yankees triumph, hoping that one or both set a new home-run standard.

A freak ailment, a hip infection caused by a doctor's injection, knocked Mickey out of the race. He cried in a Lenox Hill hospital bed when Maris hit that number 61 off Boston's Tracy Stallard, and he cried again some 25 years later when he described those events for a book on Maris by coauthor Maury Allen.

Mickey had bad legs most of his career, which cut down his mobility and probably damaged his career numbers. A World Series fly ball hit by Willie Mays in 1951 led to a knee injury when Joe DiMaggio called Mickey off a catch at the last instant. Mickey slowed himself into a Yankee Stadium drainage ditch, and that explosive speed that had made manager Casey Stengel and other observers so breathless the spring before was never there again.

He fought through those injuries and so many more until he left the game in 1968. During Mantle's final at-bat in Detroit, Tigers pitcher Denny McLain had offered up a cupcake of a pitch for a farewell homer as a simple signal of the affection even the opposition held for Mantle.

Mantle received the game's greatest honor in 1974 when he was elected to baseball's Hall of Fame. Baseball Writers' Association of America secretary-treasurer Jack Lang called Mickey at his Dallas home to inform him of his election. "Did Slick make it?" he asked of pitching pal Whitey Ford, known by that nickname for his native New York sharpness. When informed that Ford had also been elected, Mickey could then appreciate his honor. The 1974 bus ride with family and friends from New York City to Cooperstown, New York, for the Hall of Fame induction was one of the game's legendary happy outings.

The years after Mantle left the game were filled with other days of joy and a few days of disappointment and sorrow. Business ventures failed. His knees were troublesome on the golf course. Home life was difficult. A son was lost. Even pal Billy Martin was taken from him in a tragic 1989 automobile accident.

Bill Liederman, coauthor of this work, created a new and happy place. They opened a restaurant on Central Park South in Manhattan, and it soon became what Mickey had imagined: *the* sports hangout for athletes and fans. Mickey Mantle's followed Toots Shor's, where Mickey spent some joyous nights as a young Yankee, as the right place to eat, drink, and be merry for sports fans and celebrities alike. He greeted fans there, talked of all the old days, waited patiently, signed autographs, and posed for pictures with the legions of Yankee fans.

Through all his baseball accomplishments, the World Series triumphs, the 1956 Triple Crown, the stirring home-run race of 1961, the final grinding years, and the adulation he received each Old Timers' Day at Yankee Stadium and everywhere he went in New York, Mantle remained at the core a simple country kid.

He played the game because he loved it, the sounds of the bat hitting the ball, the baseball reaching his leather glove, the noise of the fans when he delivered one of the mighty wallops.

Yet, when he quit and years later, he would talk about a nightmare he had that he arrived at Yankee Stadium and couldn't get inside. That was what mattered, what really counted in his life, the games inside the Stadium. All else was just window dressing.

"You know what I miss, what I really miss?" he once told Maury Allen. "Just sitting around the clubhouse with the guys, kidding around, telling tales, sharing our experiences."

Unlike most baseball players, his status only grew as he was more removed from the game. The years marched on and his fame became greater. His standing in the American scene probably reached its zenith in his final days of 1995 as he battled the devastation of liver cancer.

He fought the disease with the same bravery, the same heroism with which he had fought the toughest pitchers in the game. He took the time to inspire others to respect their own lives, to live heartier and healthier, to appreciate each adventure.

At his Dallas funeral, broadcaster Bob Costas, who carried a Mickey Mantle rookie card in his wallet, told a tale that Mickey often told on himself.

"Mickey would say he was met at the pearly gates by St. Peter, who shook his hand and said, 'Mick, we checked the records. We know some of what went on. Sorry, we can't let you in. But before you go, God wants to know if you'd sign these six dozen baseballs,'" Costas recalled.

Mickey's impact on all the people he touched remains constant. This book is about Mickey, of course, but it is also about the people he connected with and the lasting memories that come to them when they hear the name Mickey Mantle.

Bob Sheppard is the Yankees public-address announcer, a voice heard around Yankee Stadium for more than 50 years. He is connected to Mickey by time and tone. Both Mickey and Sheppard made their first appearance at the Stadium on April 17, 1951.

Comedian Billy Crystal once said, "There are three things that are perfectly Yankee—the pinstripes, the logo, and Bob Sheppard. When I go to heaven I want Bob Sheppard to introduce me . . . the comedian . . . Billy Crystal . . . the comedian."

In his nineties now, Sheppard recalled his and Mickey's debut on the Yankees scene in 1951.

"Mickey Mantle was the perfect name," said Sheppard in that melodic voice heard around the Stadium for generations. "Both names starting with the same letter. I just loved announcing his name. And one day, shortly before he died, we were both being interviewed on a television program. All of a sudden he turned to me and said—right there on the air— that every time he heard me announce his name, he got goose bumps. And I felt the same way about announcing him."

If you were a teammate of Mickey Mantle's, a baseball opponent, a family member, a friend, a business associate, a Mickey Mantle's restaurant customer, or a memorabilia collector, the legend lives on for you.

There is a universal respect, admiration, and awe about Mickey that has lingered and lasted for more than half a century.

He was a giant of his time, all time—a figure in 20th-century America that will last as long as any of the folk figures filling America's history.

One of Maury Allen's favorite Mantle stories involves an incident that occurred in 1963.

Mickey was the most intense player Allen ever covered. He was especially sensitive to stories about his frequent injuries. In 1963 he fractured his ankle chasing a fly ball into the wall in Baltimore. After Mantle was out several months and the Yankees kept insisting he would be back shortly, Allen wrote a kidding column about the situation. He began it by saying, "There is no Mickey Mantle. He is a figment of the Yankees' imagination." It was supposed to be a joke. The next day Allen approached Mickey as he took batting practice. Mickey saw Allen coming over. Mantle turned quickly and said, "You piss me off just standing there." All Allen could do was turn away. Mickey could have some temper tantrums. Even though the remark was aimed at Allen, he had to admit he admired Mickey's style.

Lean back now, listen to Mickey laugh with his friends, and collect the memories of so many lives that were changed, thrilled, and touched by a deep, tender, or casual connection to Mickey Mantle.

# Our Mickey

CHERISHED MEMORIES OF AN
AMERICAN ICON

*For the great competitor that he was, Mick also knew how to have fun with the game and keep things light when they had to be.* Photo courtesy of Ozzie Sweet.

# Mantle as Teammate and Yankee

## WHITEY FORD

**Whitey Ford, along with Billy Martin, was Mickey's closest pal on the Yankees and in all the years afterward. Ford, a Hall of Fame left-handed pitcher, joined the team in 1950. Mickey came to the Yankees in 1951. Ford missed the 1951 and 1952 seasons while he was in the service. They were reunited in 1953 and remained the closest pals until Mickey's death in 1995. Mickey won a lot of games for Whitey with his bat and glove.**

Mickey was on the disabled list early in the sixties with a pulled groin muscle. When Whitey wasn't scheduled to pitch the next day, he would share a few cocktails with Mickey. They partied together long and hard one night in Detroit. Mickey staggered into the ballpark without any sleep and took a seat in the corner of the dugout, certain he couldn't get into the game because of being on the disabled list.

Manager Ralph Houk yelled to Mickey late in the game, "Get a bat, Mickey, you're hitting."

"I can't play, Skip," replied Mickey. "I'm on the DL."

"No, you're not," said Houk. "I took you off this morning."

Mickey staggered to the plate. The first pitch was a fastball down the middle for a strike. The second pitch was another fastball over the middle.

"Mickey told me he saw three baseballs and hit the one in the middle," said Ford.

The crowd went wild as Mickey jogged around the bases after a towering home run.

Mickey got back to the dugout and collapsed on the bench, trying to catch his breath. Ford sat down next to him and asked, "Mick, was it hard hitting that ball?"

"The hard part wasn't hitting the ball," said Mickey with his huge grin. "The hard part was getting around the bases."

---

"There was this one game that Mickey won for me in very dramatic fashion with a ninth-inning homer. After it was over all the sportswriters crowded into the clubhouse around my locker. There were always 20 or 30 around, but this game there seemed to be 50 or 60. It was a regular-season game against the Red Sox, not a World Series, but there were maybe more guys than I had ever seen at a regular-season game. I stood there for about half an hour answering all their questions. Mickey didn't see any of it. He was in the training room getting treatment for his legs.

"There was this one guy among the sportswriters, about as ugly a guy as you could imagine. Big ears, a goofy smile, a crooked nose, and a mouth that seemed to go off in two directions. I mean this guy was major-league ugly. He was new on the beat, and neither Mickey nor I really knew who he was.

"Finally, Mickey comes out and walks to his locker. I'm going in the other direction to the shower. The press crowds around Mickey like I had never seen before.

"'Hey, Mickey,' I yelled over. 'Where the hell did all these guys come from?' Mickey just flashed that famous grin of his.

"'I don't know about most of them,' said Mickey, 'but that one guy'—as he quickly nodded toward the ugly sportswriter—'he came from Barnum and Bailey.' Nobody was quicker with one-liners than Mickey.

"We were sitting in the lobby of the hotel in Detroit. I was with Mickey and our backup catcher, Darrell Johnson, who later became a real good manager. We looked over to the side and there were two guys dressed in suits and ties, real stiff like, and trying to hide behind newspapers. Mickey noticed them right away. I told Mickey I knew who they were: detectives. George Weiss, the Yankee GM, had decided that we were staying out late too much, me and Mickey, and he wanted to catch us in a bad place and fine us and embarrass us. Me and Mickey decided to play a joke on these guys. We walked slowly out of the hotel lobby and hailed a cab. We looked behind and these guys were out the door and they were getting into a cab. We told the driver to go around a few blocks and then come back to the hotel. He did that about five or six times. The bill was maybe five or six bucks in those days, but we were laughing all the way as the cab with the cops kept turning as we turned. Finally, we got out in front of the hotel and walked back to our seats. Just then Tony Kubek and Bobby Richardson showed up in the lobby, and they started walking down the street. The cops followed them. Tony and Bobby, the two straightest guys on the team, walked down to the nearby YMCA. They played Ping-Pong for about an hour. Then they walked back toward the hotel. The cops followed them. Tony and Bobby made one stop. They walked into an ice cream store. Bobby ordered a chocolate cone and Tony ordered vanilla. That was the wildest thing any of us did that day. Mickey always loved that story after it came out in the papers. Weiss was the guy who was embarrassed. Mickey loved that."

Whitey and Mickey were as close as two friends could possibly ever be. When Whitey's daughter had a baby many years ago, Whitey's son-in-law called the Ford home shortly after the baby's birth in the middle of the night. He reported that the baby was beautiful, Whitey's daughter was fine, and the entire family was thrilled.

Whitey picked up the telephone and called Mickey in Dallas. "Mick, Mick, you're not gonna believe this," Ford shouted over the phone. "Last night, for the first time in my life, I slept with a grandmother."

## JIM BOUTON

**In the sixties, Jim Bouton was an All-Star pitcher. He was a Yankees rookie in 1962, won 21 games in 1963, and won 18 in 1964. He also won two World Series games against the Cardinals in 1964, including one in which Mickey Mantle homered off Barney Schultz for the win. Bouton was 62–63 in a 10-year career that lasted from 1962 until 1978 with some years off to nurse a sore arm, play amateur baseball, and write maybe baseball's best book ever, the iconoclastic *Ball Four*. In the seventies he was a TV sportscaster, wrote a sequel to *Ball Four* entitled *I'm Glad You Didn't Take It Personally*, and acted in a movie called *The Long Goodbye*. He made a brief comeback with the Atlanta Braves in 1978. His first novel, *Strike Zone*, cowritten with Eliot Asinof, was published in 1994. Bouton is now a businessman and motivational speaker, and he lives in Massachusetts with his wife, Paula Kurman.**

"I won my first game in the big leagues with a shutout against the Washington Senators. I did a radio interview after

*Mick's teammates loved his ability to have a good time.*
*Mickey probably got a lot more laughs than fish on this trip*
*with Billy Martin.* Photo courtesy of Ozzie Sweet.

the game, and when I came into the clubhouse about 15 minutes later I opened the door to see Mickey Mantle putting down the last towel on the floor like a magic carpet for me."

---

Until 1998, Jim Bouton was never invited back for Old Timers' Day. This was very hurtful to him because he felt he was entitled to stand next to the other Yankees greats and bathe in the crowd's applause along with them. Secretly, he suspected Mickey had put the kibosh on his appearance because he was still pissed off at him about *Ball Four*. He couldn't have been more off base.

"Back in 1994, when Mickey Mantle's son Billy died, I had sent Mickey a brief note saying how bad I felt for him. I said I had a nice memory of Billy, a polite little boy, running around the Yankees' clubhouse during spring training. I also said I hoped Mickey was feeling better about *Ball Four*, that I had never intended to hurt him, and that I looked back on my Yankee years as the greatest years of my life.

"I never expected to hear back from Mickey; I just wanted him to have the note. But about two weeks later I walked into my office and my secretary was standing by the answering machine with an enigmatic smile on her face. She said there was a message I should play for myself. I punched the button.

"'Jim, this is Mickey,' said that familiar voice. 'I just got your letter about . . . you know, saying you're sorry about Billy, and I appreciate it. And I never was really hurt by your book, I think that's been exaggerated a lot . . . and I sure in the hell never did tell the Yankees that if you came to an Old Timers' Game, or something, I wasn't going to come; I heard that was out. Anyway, thanks for the letter, and everything's fine with me. Thanks a lot, Bud.'"

---

"I lost my daughter, Laurie, in an automobile accident in 1997. My son, Michael, wrote a letter to *The New York Times* in 1998 asking that I be invited back to Old Timers' Day. I finally got a call that I was invited back—No. 56, the Bulldog, back in the Stadium. It was very thrilling. I think it all started when Mickey made it known that he had nothing against me."

## MEL STOTTLEMYRE

**Mel Stottlemyre came to the Yankees as a rookie up from their Richmond farm club in August of 1964. The Yankees were in a tough pennant race, and Stottlemyre went 9–3 the rest of that season and was given a great deal of credit for the Yankees' come-from-behind victory. He also won a World Series game against the Cardinals.**

"I remembered the first day I arrived at the Stadium, a frightened kid, just overwhelmed—22 years old, and here I was walking into the clubhouse at the famous Yankee Stadium. I was pointed to my locker by Pete Sheehy, the clubhouse guy, and I started to change into my uniform. The Yankees had a tradition in those days that they didn't get very friendly with a new guy because he might not be around very long. I was kind of shy and didn't push myself on anybody even in the minor leagues. I put on my uniform facing the wall, and nobody came near me. I think I was just straightening my hat and getting ready to go on the field for the first time in a Yankee uniform. A guy came over and I heard him say hello and welcome to the club. I looked up and it was Mickey Mantle. I couldn't even tell you how big that was to me. We became very close friends. Not a day goes by that I don't think about Mickey and miss him."

## BOBBY COX

**Bobby Cox joined the Yankees as a platoon third baseman in 1968. It was Mickey Mantle's final year as a player. Cox had one more season in the big leagues. Then he went to the minors and became a manager at the Yankees' farm at Fort Lauderdale in 1971. He started as a manager with the Atlanta Braves in 1978, moved to Toronto in 1982, returned as general manager in 1986 in Atlanta, and resumed managing the team in 1990. He has more post-season wins than any manager in baseball history.**

---

"I remember when I first came up to the Yankees and I started Opening Day in 1968," Cox said. "I was so nervous I could hardly stand. I leaned forward on my toes as they played the National Anthem. I thought I might pull a muscle. Mickey Mantle was out there in center field. He had always been my hero. I couldn't believe I was standing on the same field with Mickey as a teammate. Mickey was always so friendly and funny to be around. I knew he was hurting and this figured to be his last season. I wanted to remember it. I waited several weeks. I finally asked the PR guy, Marty Appel, if he could ask Mickey if he would pose for a picture with me. I was too nervous to ask Mickey myself. The next day Mickey just walked over, put his arm around my shoulder, and smiled. The Yankee team photographer walked up. He shot the picture. From that day until this one, it has followed me everywhere I have gone—me and Mickey, wow."

## MOOSE SKOWRON

**Bill "Moose" Skowron was the Yankees first baseman from 1954 through 1962. He batted .282 over 14 years and was always close to Mickey.**

*Mickey poses with teammates (from left) Billy Martin, Hank Bauer, Bill "Moose" Skowron, Yogi Berra, and Jerry Coleman. Whitey was probably playing golf that day.*
Photo courtesy of AP/Wide World Photos.

"Whenever we had to have a big hit to win a game it seemed Mickey won it for us. He was just such a great player, the greatest I ever played with. He got a little mad when he had a bad day or we lost. But he always came back fast. It always hurt me to watch how much he suffered with those bad legs and everything, pulling off those bandages and unwrapping himself after every game. He was just so much fun to be around. I wish he was still around. He used to make a lot of money for me by making sure I got paid good money when we did any of those card shows. They really only wanted Mickey, but if me and Hank [Bauer] and Johnny [Blanchard] came along, he saw that it was a good payday for us.

"Mickey liked to kid me about my haircut and my nickname. I always wore a short crew cut. He thought that was funny. He always called me Billmoose, like the cartoon character Bullmoose. I used to kid him when he liked to sleep on the training table after a long night. They got a lot of good players in the game today. They ain't got no Mickey Mantle."

## BOBBY RICHARDSON

**Bobby Richardson was the Yankees second baseman from 1955 through 1966 when he suddenly retired at the age of 31. He was a teammate of Mickey Mantle's all those years and, despite their different attitudes about life and different personalities, they became close friends.**

"Mickey would come down to visit with us almost every winter in South Carolina, and we would go out hunting and have lots of laughs. I delivered the eulogy when Roger Maris died in 1985 in his hometown of Fargo, North Dakota. Mickey was there, and when it was over he was in tears and came up to me and said, 'Bobby, I want you to do that for me.' I told him I would. Then when Mickey died in 1995 I delivered his eulogy in Dallas. I made him a promise at Roger's funeral. I just didn't think it would be that soon.

"Mickey and I bought a vacation house together on Grandfather Mountain in Boone County, South Carolina. It is a beautiful resort area. We used to go there every winter when we were playing to hunt and fish together. We invited other guys from the Yankees down, and we just had so much fun being together, replaying some of the games and talking about the guys on our team and other teams.

"I didn't party with Mickey, but I really enjoyed his company. He was an incredibly warm and funny guy. Sometimes my wife and our kids would come down [Richardson now has 15 grandchildren] and you could see how much Mickey enjoyed being around them. It was all so relaxing for him after the season and after all the attention paid to him throughout the year.

"One year after Mickey was retired he came down to my home in Sumter for a YMCA fund-raiser. He was just great with the people. They were just crazy about him. We arranged for a little hitting clinic on a local field. Tony Kubek flew down from Wisconsin to be with us to pitch to Mickey. He kidded around and threw change-ups and curveballs to Mickey, and Mickey just swung and missed. One time he actually twisted his foot and that was the end of the hitting. That made Mickey mad. We played a little game for the people with the college kids and a few American Legion players, and Tony hit a huge home run over the deepest part of the field. That made Mickey even madder.

"One other time we had a fund-raiser on the campus of the University of South Carolina. I coached there for many years and retired in 1990. Mickey got two thousand bats with his name on them sent down there to be sold for the charity event and even signed about two hundred of them under his printed name. What a thrill that was for the people.

"There were always such crowds around Mickey. He was so recognizable wherever he went. One time we had a little charity event and Mickey was on the field showing kids how to hit, and everybody started crowding up the little stands we had. After a while there were so many people pushing and shoving in the stands that the wooden structure broke.

"Lew Fonseca, the famous baseball film producer, made a film of Mickey's life, and we showed it to the kids at the school. It showed Mickey hitting, running, making those great catches, and just generally performing as he did for so many years. Mickey loved the film, and I have used it as a training film for our teams for many years.

"It's hard to believe Mickey is gone almost 10 years now. I think about him all the time. Whenever I go to a charity event or a golf outing with some of the guys his name comes up. Somebody always has a story about him.

"I probably shouldn't tell you this, but one time we had Roger Maris down here for an event and we went out to dinner that night. We were having a wonderful evening and nobody bothered us. I overheard somebody, talking in a whisper, as they looked over, saying, 'Hey, that guy looks like Roger Maris.' That wouldn't happen with Mickey. He was one of a kind."

## PHIL LINZ

**Phil Linz was a backup infielder with the Yankees for four seasons from 1962 through 1965. He had two humorous memories of his time with Mickey Mantle as a teammate.**

---

"[It was] the first year I joined the club and we were playing in Detroit. After the game Mickey came over to me and asked if I wanted to join him for dinner. Mickey Mantle. Wow. What a thrill. I said I certainly did.

He gave me an address of a restaurant and told me to meet him there about 7:00. We were off that day and I spent most of the afternoon thinking about it and getting ready. I jumped in a cab and gave the guy the name and the address. He looked at me sort of funny and then he took off.

"We just kept riding and riding and riding. I was getting a little sick just looking at the meter. We finally slowed down after a $40 cab ride. I paid him and then I looked up.

"This place was in a broken-down neighborhood, holes in the walls, people sleeping in the street. Real bad. I walked in to this place very cautiously. I saw nothing but minority people, all having lots to drink. I asked if Mickey was there. The guy didn't understand me. It was real scary. I decided to leave. I walked a few blocks until I was able to see another cab. Then I got back to the hotel glad I was alive.

"The next day I walk into the clubhouse. Mickey is there. 'Hey, Linz, where were you? I waited all night.' Then everybody started laughing. I knew I had been had."

———————

Linz's other story with Mickey took place on a team bus after a bitter loss in Chicago.

"I had bought this harmonica. Then I started playing it. Frank Crosetti, an old-time Yankee coach, got real mad. He told me to stop playing. I just started to play softly. Then Yankee manager Yogi Berra came to the back of the bus. He started shouting. I didn't know what he said. Mickey was sitting behind me. I asked him. Mickey answered, 'He said to play louder.' I did. Then Yogi asked for the harmonica. I threw it at him and he threw it back. It hit Joe Pepitone. The press made a big deal out of it, and I was fined $200 by Yogi. I didn't care. I got paid $10,000 by the harmonica company for a commercial. I owed it all to Mickey."

## CLETE BOYER

**Clete Boyer, one of the baseball-playing Boyers of
Missouri, was a teammate of Mickey's from 1959 through
1966. Boyer played 16 years in the big leagues, hit 162
home runs, and was one of the finest-fielding third base-
men in the history of the game.**

---

"I always used to have these contests with Mickey in batting practice for who could hit a ball farther. I liked to hit
long balls over the walls in BP. Nobody could do it better than
Mickey. We started out doing it for sodas. I won once in a
while. Then we started betting a few bucks on it. I never won
after that. I think Mickey made a living off me.

"I ran with Mickey a lot. He was always so much fun. I
just can't tell you all we did. Just say that we had a lot of
laughs. He was a great friend, a real brother to me, as tight as
my real brothers. I learned so much baseball and so much life
from Mickey. He was the best I ever saw."

## TOM TRESH

**Tom Tresh played with Mickey Mantle from 1961 through
1968. He batted .245 in a nine-year big-league career.**

---

"I was a switch-hitter, so when I came up they compared
me to Mickey. Nobody could be compared to Mickey. He was
the best and the only one of his kind. I don't know if it hurt
my career or not, but I did try to hit home runs like Mickey
did. It just couldn't happen. It was just the greatest baseball
experience of a lot of lives on the Yankees to play on the same
team with Mickey Mantle. We not only respected him as the
game's greatest player, we loved him as a man. How did we

*Martin, Mantle, and Ford were often summoned to
"Judge" Casey Stengel's courtroom for their misdeeds
off the field, as depicted in this Bill Gallo cartoon.*

show it? We named children after him. I have a Mickey Tresh.
I know about a dozen other Yankees who have kids named
after him. I think there are Mickey Gibbs, Mickey Bahnsen,
Mickey Cumberland, Mickey Closter, and so many more."

## PHIL RIZZUTO

**Hall of Famer Phil Rizzuto played shortstop for the
Yankees from 1941 through 1956 with three seasons out
for World War II service in the navy. He was the 1950
American League MVP when he hit .324 and scored 125
runs. He broadcast Yankees baseball for 40 years after his
playing days ended.**

---

"Holy cow, when I think of Mickey I just think of those
huge home runs he hit. He was the strongest guy I ever saw,
and he could hit a ball farther than anybody I ever saw. But he
was also a great guy around the clubhouse. Always laughing
and making fun. Even when I became a broadcaster he never
stopped having fun with me. In 1961, in that home-run year,
he hid my hat on a cold day, and then I got on the team bus
and he was wearing it.

"I heard all this talk about the kid shortstop the Yankees
were bringing up in 1951. I was worried about losing my job.
That's the way I was. I always worried about losing my job.
Then we went to spring training and I saw this kid, Mantle,
working out. He didn't have the coordination to be an infielder, and he had that great arm. The only trouble was he
would throw most of the balls from shortstop into the stands.
The people out there in Arizona that spring made sure they
sat far away from first base. Mickey was scaring a lot of people
in those early workouts. After a few days I decided I didn't
have to worry about my job.

"He was a great kid and we got real friendly in a hurry after the first season. I loved to be around him because he was so much fun. He was always laughing and liked to do and say funny things in the clubhouse. I'll tell you what I didn't like about him. On the field he would get together with Billy Martin and put things in my glove. In those days we left our gloves on the field, and sometimes I would go out there in the fifth or sixth inning, pick up my glove, and start howling. They would scream because they had put a rubber snake in my glove or some crawling caterpillar. I could have killed them. One time Mickey put a squishy hot dog inside the fingers of a glove. When I went on the field and put the glove on I felt it and threw it in the air. Mickey was laughing hysterically.

"Well, in 1956, the Yankees picked up Enos Slaughter so they could have another left-handed hitter for the World Series against Brooklyn. George Weiss [the GM] and Casey called me into the office and began going over the roster. They wanted to know who I thought we should drop to make room on the roster for Slaughter. I came up with three or four names and they knocked each of them down. 'No, we need that extra lefty or we need that backup third catcher.' I finally got the message it was me they were dropping. I couldn't believe it."

"That really hurt me to see Phil go," Mickey said in a later interview. "I knew that if it could happen to him it could happen to anybody. It could happen to me."

## BOBBY MURCER

**Bobby Murcer is from Oklahoma City. He started as a Yankees shortstop and was moved to center field just the way his hero, Mickey Mantle, started with the Yankees and was moved to the outfield. Murcer joined the Yankees in 1965 and was a teammate and close pal of Mantle's. He hit**

**252 home runs in a 17-year career with the Yankees, Giants, and Cubs. The press always compared them, but except for the shortstop-to-center-field and Oklahoma background they were unalike. Mickey helped ease Murcer through the pressures of this comparison.**

---

"Mickey always told me to be myself. He reminded me that he went through the same thing when he broke in and they compared him with [Joe] DiMaggio. That really helped. Nobody could hit a ball like Mickey could. He was going downhill when I joined the club, but he was still the most powerful hitter in the game. We became close friends and remained so to the end. There was nobody like Mickey in the game. He was a wonderful player and a fantastic friend. I will always love Mickey.

"Tradition by position, that's what some of the players called it, you know, center field where Joe DiMaggio played and then Mickey and then me. Like right field with the Babe and first base with Lou Gehrig. Anyway, I loved playing center field for the Yankees and was honored to be out there. Then in 1974 [manager] Bill Virdon moved me to right and put Elliott Maddox in center field. That broke my heart. Mickey was from Oklahoma. I was from Oklahoma. Mickey was the Yankees center fielder. I was the Yankees center fielder. Then one day I wasn't. It was the saddest day of my baseball life. Well, maybe second saddest. They traded me away from the Yankees. *That* was the saddest."

## WILLIE RANDOLPH

**Willie Randolph played 18 years in the big leagues with a .276 lifetime average. He was an exceptional second baseman and a leader on the Yankees teams of the seventies and eighties. He is currently the bench coach of the Yankees.**

"I grew up in Brooklyn in the Brownsville section. We went to Yankee Stadium in the sixties as part of a program called the Con Ed Kids. We sat deep in the bleachers and yelled from our seats at Mickey Mantle in center field. Every so often he would take his cap off and wave back at us. When I became a Yankee and met him as a spring-training instructor I told him that. He always said, 'Nah, I wouldn't do that.' He just didn't want to admit it."

## JOE PEPITONE

**Joe Pepitone hit .258 in 12 big-league seasons. He was a Yankee from 1962 through 1969. His wild habits kept him from superstardom. He hit 219 homers, played first base, and moved to the outfield when Mickey Mantle was switched to first base in 1967. He now works in the Yankees' community relations department.**

"I joined the Yankees in 1962. I became the regular first baseman in 1963. We played the Dodgers in the World Series that year. Mickey kept telling me it would be my fault if we didn't win. I was the only change in the lineup from the Yankee team that won in 1962. Then I made that error when I lost [Clete] Boyer's throw in the white shirts. Mickey never stopped kidding me about that after we lost.

"When I moved to center field I wanted to play out there like Mickey. I pulled up my pants and hit like Mickey. Only I couldn't hit them as far or as often as he did. It was great playing with the Yankees. It was greater playing with Mickey."

## YOGI BERRA

**Yogi Berra hit .285 with 358 home runs in a Hall of Fame Yankees career from 1946 through 1963. He managed the Yankees to a pennant in 1964 and played four more games with the Mets in 1965 before becoming a coach for former Yankees manager Casey Stengel. Berra managed the Mets from 1972 through 1975, including a 1973 pennant, and managed the Yankees again in 1984 and 1985. He was a teammate of Mickey Mantle's from 1951 through 1963 and managed Mantle in 1964.**

———————————

"We were playing in Boston one day and Mickey said calling a game was easy. He said he could do it from center field. I said we could try it. Whitey [Ford] was pitching. So when Mickey stood up straight in center field I called the fastball. If he bent over I called the curveball. If he wiggled his glove I called a change-up for Whitey. We were leading 2–0 into the seventh inning. Mickey came into the dugout and laughed, 'I've carried you as far as I can. You're on your own the rest of the way.' So I called the pitches and we won the game 2–0. Mickey was great to play with on and off the field. Once in a while we'd go out and have a few pops. I'd look at my watch and when it got to 11:30 at night I'd get up and go. 'I'm catching tomorrow.' Mickey and Billy and Whitey would stay late. It never seemed to bother them."

## HANK BAUER

**Hank Bauer played for the Yankees from 1948 through 1959 after combat service with the marines in the South Pacific in World War II. He played in nine World Series with the Yankees and managed Kansas City and Baltimore.**

*Mickey waves to the Yankee Stadium crowd as he and close pal Whitey Ford are joined by Ron Guidry and Reggie Jackson at an Old Timers' Day.*
Photo courtesy of Barton Silverman.

"I remember when Mickey joined us in 1951. He hit all those home runs, [18] in spring training, and you could see he was some kind of a young player. He used to strike out a lot, too. He could hit a ball over the roof and he could bunt the next time up for a base hit. One time he hit a ground ball and the second baseman bobbled it. Mickey didn't run. He was mad about that pitch. He thought he should have hit it over the roof. When he came back to the bench I looked at him hard and yelled at him, 'Don't fool with my money.' Only I didn't say 'fool' and he got the message. I don't think he ever did that again."

## MIKE HEGAN

**Mike Hegan is a Cleveland Indians broadcaster who finished his 15th season with the Tribe in 2003 after 12 years as a broadcaster with the Milwaukee Brewers. He played in the big leagues for 12 years and was Mickey Mantle's backup first baseman with the Yankees in 1967.**

"My roommate that year was Thad Tillotson, one of the team's pitchers. He was a pretty good golfer, and he used to brag about how good he was all the time. One day in spring training he challenged Mickey and Whitey Ford, and after the workout they went out with us. We bet a few bucks on each hole, and by the time we finished we owed them a hundred bucks.

"That was a lot of money for kids like us. Mickey finally said we didn't have to pay but he hoped we learned a lesson that rookies like us shouldn't be challenging the vets in anything."

## BILLY MARTIN

**Billy Martin joined the Yankees as a backup infielder in 1950. He became one of manager Casey Stengel's favorites. He and Mickey became the closest of friends. In one of baseball's most famous on-again, off-again love/hate relationships of all time with Yankees owner George Steinbrenner, Martin managed the Yankees five different times. He died in an auto accident on Christmas day in 1989 after spending most of the afternoon drinking with a pal at a local watering hole in upstate New York.**

---

"I remember when I first met Mickey," Martin said many years ago. "It was in the spring of 1951 and this kid was with us from the minors. I just walked over to him and said, 'Hi, Pardner.' I knew he was from Oklahoma. Mickey just looked down on the ground and whispered, 'Mantle.' I told him I knew who he was. I read the sports pages every day and there was a lot already written about him. I don't think anyone will ever forget his name."

## TOMMY HENRICH

**Tommy Henrich, at 91, is still one of the best-remembered and most-revered Yankees. He joined the team in 1937 and retired after the 1950 season. He was nicknamed "Old Reliable" for hitting so well in the clutch.**

---

"I worked as an outfield coach for the Yankees in Mickey's first year, 1951, which was Joe's [DiMaggio] last year. I could see this incredible ability right away in Mantle. You can teach finesse in the game, positioning, how to get a jump on the ball. You can't teach physical things, how to hit a ball hard, how to throw hard, how to run fast. That's God given, that's all. When he showed up, everybody knew it. Mickey had it. You could see that in a second. You would have to be a fool not to recognize his talent."

## GEORGE SELKIRK

**George Selkirk, a Yankee from 1934 to 1942 and later a baseball executive, may have had the toughest job in the history of baseball. He replaced Babe Ruth as the Yankees' right fielder. Selkirk was the manager of the Yankees' farm club, the Kansas City Blues, in 1951.**

---

"Casey [Stengel] sent Mickey down to us after he started striking out a lot. As soon as he joined us I told him just to relax. You could see the talent, but he was just so tight. He couldn't get comfortable. Then one day he called his father and said he wanted to go home. When his dad arrived they had a big talk and his father frightened Mickey into staying. He said he didn't want a quitter in his family. Mickey stayed with us, and soon he was hitting those balls a mile. His dad died soon after that 1951 season. I always wondered what kind of a player and what kind of a man Mickey might have become if he had his dad alongside him all those years."

## ART DITMAR

**Art Ditmar pitched for the New York Yankees from 1957 through 1961. He pitched in the World Series for the Yankees in 1957, 1958, and 1960.**

---

"I enjoyed playing with the Yankees. It was the best part of my career. It was always exciting over there because we were always in the pennant race and the fans were worked up in every game. Winning is the greatest thrill you can get in the game, and I won almost every year I was with them.

"You know what was almost as much fun? Watching Mickey Mantle play every day. I always felt that when Mickey was hot we won. It was as simple as that. Mickey hits and we move. If Mickey doesn't hit, we aren't going anyplace. He hit most of the time, so we won all those pennants with the Yankees."

## RALPH HOUK

**Ralph Houk played for the Yankees as a backup catcher from 1947 through 1954 after a heroic World War II career as a U.S. Ranger major—later his baseball nickname. The Major managed the Yankees from 1961 through 1964, served as general manager, and then managed the Yankees one last time from 1966 through 1973. He later managed Detroit.**

---

"The first time I saw Mickey is what I remember most. It was spring training in Phoenix and they brought Mickey to camp as a 19-year-old kid. He hit the ball so hard it was unreal. Each time up he just seemed to hit it harder than the time before. He was hitting the rookie pitchers early, the guys just trying to make the club. Then he started hitting the regular pitchers—you know, those guys who had pitched on all the Yankee winners. Then he started clubbing the opposing pitchers when the games started. It got so that batting practice and Mickey's game at-bats were the most exciting part of the

*Mickey and Billy off on one of their postseason hunting trips, after wrapping up another pennant and World Series title.* Photo courtesy of the Mantle family.

day. No matter what else was going on—running drills, sliding, fielding practice, just conditioning—it would all stop when Mickey walked into the cage to bat left-handed or right-handed. I mean there was never anything like it. You talk about exciting players. Well, as far as I'm concerned, there was Mickey—and then there was the rest of them.

"I called Mickey into my office the day spring training began in 1961," Houk recalled. "We talked about the prospects for the team after we had won the year before but lost the Series to Pittsburgh. That really hurt Mickey. I knew it wouldn't be a successful season unless we went all the way and won the Series. I told that to Mickey. Then I said, 'You have to be the leader of the team.' Mickey looked at me funny and just sort of mumbled, 'How do I do that?' I told him he just had to be himself. He could lead by playing hard his own way. That would inspire everybody else. I guess it worked. Mickey helped Roger in that home-run season, we won the pennant, and we won the World Series over Cincinnati pretty easily. That's what I call leadership."

## ROGER MARIS

**Roger Maris broke the single-season home-run record of Babe Ruth in 1961 with 61 homers. It was the most pressure-packed season any player experienced in baseball history with the chase of Ruth, the controversy over doing it in 154 games (as Babe had) or 162 as was the new schedule, the so-called asterisk ordered by Commissioner Ford Frick, and the challenge against his own teammate, Mantle, who had now become a Yankees icon.**

"That year was incredible," Maris said in a book about his life written with Maury Allen. "It was a great rivalry on the field, me and Mickey, but we were great friends in every other way. Heck, we even lived together for a while that season. I think I remember the day Mickey really became my pal. We each had maybe 25–30 home runs and the press was jumping on the story. Every day was a big deal whether I hit one or not. I went two or three days without hitting a homer. Then we were in a tough game and I was up with a couple of guys on. I got jammed on the pitch and just popped it up. The fans started giving it to me. They were booing me for not hitting a home run and they were booing me for not getting a big hit at this time. Nobody felt worse than me. As I walked by Mickey he just gave me that smile of his and asked, 'Hey, you trying to steal my fans?' That made me laugh. Mickey had been booed plenty in Yankee Stadium. He understood what it was like to go through that. I think that relaxed me and really helped me."

## JERRY COLEMAN

**Jerry Coleman has been in baseball more than half a century—as a player for the Yankees, a front-office executive, a scout, a manager, and a broadcaster. His fondest time in the game was as Mickey Mantle's roommate.**

"I was his secretary, not his roommate. The phone never stopped ringing while we were on the road. It was this friend of Mickey's or this guy with a business deal or this relative or even an old teammate just calling to say hello. Mickey never wanted to talk to anybody, so my job was to get rid of them in a nice way. One time Mickey came back to the room early in the morning after a long night. I could see he needed some rest before the game. He wouldn't make the team bus. He'd come out by himself and I was in charge of telling [manager] Casey Stengel. Just before I left, the phone rang. This time Mickey picked it up. I don't know why. He got a smile on his face and said, 'I'll see you at the ballpark, Pardner.' That was his way of telling me he wanted me out of the room and wanted the room for himself. So I just left. The game was maybe a half hour away from starting and Mickey finally showed up. He was all smiles. He knew Casey would fine him, but I guess he thought it was worth it. Casey could see he wasn't in any shape to play. But there was his name in the lineup. Maybe Casey was just trying to show him up and embarrass him. Anyway the game started and the first time up he hit one out left-handed. He struck out a couple of times and then he hit one out right-handed as we won the game. I've been around this game a long time. There was never anyone like Mickey. He was an amazing player and an amazing man. I got a few big hits in the game and made a few good plays, but my greatest thrill was being Mickey's roommate."

## BOBBY BROWN

**Bobby Brown played eight seasons for the Yankees from 1946 through 1954. He batted .279 as a part-time player but hit .439 as his average in four World Series. Brown retired as a player at the age of 29 to finish his residency as a cardiologist. He became one of the most prominent physicians around Fort Worth, Texas. He later returned to baseball as president of the American League.**

The favorite story most everyone told about Bobby Brown concerned his days as Yogi Berra's roommate. They both were staying up late reading. Brown had his head buried in a medical book. Berra was leafing through a comic book. Each put their books down about the same time and Yogi, before the lights went out, asked, "How did yours come out?"

"When Bobby Brown left the game, he left with no regrets. He retired in 1954, still a young man, his future bright and promising," Mantle wrote in his autobiography *The Mick: An American Hero: The Legend and the Glory* with Herb Gluck (Doubleday), published in 1985. "Of those I played with, I think his [Bobby Brown's] situation came closest to mine, in the sense that his father always wanted him to play baseball, was always on him to do better, working tirelessly to prepare him for the majors. The same devotion as my dad's—'Goddamn, how could you have swung at that pitch?' Once Bobby had a lousy night at the Stadium. They were driving across the Washington Bridge into New Jersey and Bobby's moaning, 'Oh I feel awful. I was terrible.' When they came to the middle of the bridge, his father pulled over and stopped. He said, 'Why don't you jump?'

"It shows what can happen when you get totally wrapped up in dreams about somebody else's future. They become your own. And that's the kind of background Bobby had, same as mine, in so far as father-son relationships go.

"Bobby and I had another thing in common. When he played for the Yankees his uniform was No. 6. He spent most of 1952 and all of 1953 in military service. I wore No. 6. When he returned they gave me No. 7, gave Bobby back No. 6 and I wore No. 7 until the day I retired."

No one, of course, will ever wear No. 7 again for the Yankees, since Mantle's uniform number was retired in 1969 after he quit that spring training.

"Bobby handled a bat pretty good and only a few others could match him as a pinch-hitter. I won't mention his abilities at third base. I'd rather quote Casey again. 'Bobby reminds me of a fella who's been hitting twelve years and fielding one.'"

Casey Stengel had a great sense of describing so many things by the calendar. He would often say of a deceased teammate and friend, "He's dead at the present time."

When he came to the Mets he once looked at four or five of the young players on the field and sensed that in a few

*Mickey and Roger Maris reunited at Yankee Stadium.* Photo courtesy of the New York Yankees.

years they would be big leaguers. However, about one player, a young catcher named Greg Goossen, Casey said, "Look at him. In 10 years, he'll be 30."

"However," Mantle continued about teammate Bobby Brown, "there's no question that his hands worked wonders in another profession. After retiring from the game, he took a hospital internship, then went on to Fort Worth, where he gained national recognition as a cardiologist, and completed the circle by coming back to baseball as president of the American League. Yes, an exceptional human being."

## DAVID HALBERSTAM

**David Halberstam is a Pulitzer prize–winning author and reporter and the author of 15 books, including *The Best and the Brightest, The Powers That Be, The Reckoning, Summer of '49, October 1964,* and *The Teammates.* David's last 10 books have made *The New York Times* best-seller list. The following excerpt is taken from *October 1964* by David Halberstam, courtesy of Villard Books. Here, the author sets up the scene and establishes the tone of the Yankees locker room in 1964.**

---

"From the start, Pepitone, in particular, ignored the team hierarchy. If the normally unapproachable DiMaggio walked into the locker room, it was Pepitone who might yell out, 'Hey, Clipper, how are you? Do you want to have dinner tonight?' To everyone's amazement this seemed to please DiMaggio. It was Pepitone who, when asked by Mantle to bring him a beer, demanded that Mantle bring *him* a beer, which seemed to amuse Mantle as well. It quickly became clear that Pepitone loved Mantle, loved being Mantle's pal and basking in his reflected glory; in fact, Pepitone wanted nothing so much as to be Mantle's caddy. One or two of the older players thought there was a certain desperate quality to Pepitone's clowning, and his need for Mantle's approval. In the locker room, Pepi always had his eye on Mantle, watching to see if the great star approved of what he was doing. Some were reminded of school days, when an insecure and not particularly popular kid wanted to win favor with the most popular boy in the class.

"Generally Pepitone was successful in his attempts to charm Mantle. Pepitone, an amused Mantle said at the time, was 'the freshest rookie I ever saw,' but he also had a quick bat, a good swing, and could play both first and the outfield. Pepitone loved it when Mantle nicknamed him 'Pepinose' (Stengel, in those days before ethnic slurs were taboo, called him 'Pepperoni') and was thrilled when Mantle told a sportswriter that Pepitone was the key to the 1963 season. 'I figure we'll win by a nose,' Mantle said. Yet even the easygoing Mantle, a player always looking to be amused, thought there were times when Pepitone overstepped the bounds. Once, during batting practice, Pepitone jumped into the batting cage and got ready to take his swings when Mantle wanted to take extra swings because he wasn't hitting well. 'Five swings, Slick,' Pepitone said to an astonished and then enraged Mantle. The two exchanged sharp words and even though Pepitone was embarrassed to have done the unthinkable, to have provoked his idol, he was in too deep and could not back down. Much to his regret, he heard himself telling Mantle to get to the ballpark earlier if he wanted a few extra swings, and not to hold up his teammates. It was not, as far as Mantle was concerned, a small matter, and he did not speak to Pepitone for several weeks, leaving Pepi increasingly dispirited and desperate.

"Somehow, even the goofiest things he [Mantle] did with his teammates always seemed funny; if he raffled off tickets for $10 each on a ham, and in the end there was no ham for the winner, no one got angry. 'Well, I said you guys were taking a chance and you took a chance,' he would explain. If the team returned to La Guardia at 3:00 A.M. after a long road trip and he and Whitey Ford offered to lead the other players to the bus but instead mischievously took them on an endless tour of the labyrinth of tunnels beneath the airport, it was considered by all to be some marvelous experience: Mickey and Whitey being Mickey and Whitey, and everyone else being allowed in as their pals. He loved inviting Joe Pepitone, who longed to be his buddy, to meet him at restaurants that were not only hard to get to, but which, on occasion, did not exist.

"If a young television reporter came to interview him before a game, Mantle might give a long, seemingly serious discourse on how, when the wind was blowing in, he would try to swing with topspin so that the ball would not hang up there for the outfielders to get, while *if the wind was behind him, he would hit with backspin so that the wind would carry it farther, over the distant fence.* It was all done for the benefit of his teammates, who he knew were watching in the clubhouse and were breaking up.

"If a young black rookie joined the team and he was in the shower for the first time, Mantle might give him a quick scan to see whether the reports of black sexual endowment were true, and he would yell to Ford, 'Hey, Whitey, take a look. It's OK—he's just like us. No bigger.'

"Mantle's jokes were never mean or humiliating, for he had an instinct to include, rather than to exclude. When Jake Gibbs, the rookie catcher from Ole Miss, showed up wearing loud, black-and-orange argyle socks, Mantle asked him if there were a lot of rattlesnakes in Mississippi. When Gibbs said yes, Mantle told him that it was OK to change socks now, there were no rattlesnakes in New York and he didn't need to wear those socks to scare them off—which at once had everyone laughing and at the same time managed to make Gibbs feel more a part of the team. Mantle's great gift, Phil Linz said years later, was to tell the worst jokes in the world but somehow make them seem enormously funny."

## JOHNNY BLANCHARD

**Johnny Blanchard was a teammate of Mickey's and a valuable backup catcher for the Yanks. In 1961, he hit a .305 average in the regular season, .400 in the World Series, and cracked 21 home runs in a limited role. After retirement, Johnny remained close to Mickey, joining him on the road for card shows and coaching at Mickey's fantasy baseball camp in Fort Lauderdale. Mickey would often turn down a lucrative appearance fee if Johnny, Hank, and Moose were not included.**

———————

"It was 1961, and there were so many stars on that team; Mickey, Roger, Whitey, Yogi, the whole crew. We arrived in New York from spring training eager to open the season.

"All the players are sitting in the locker room, dressing for the game. From the far end of the locker room, Whitey calls out, 'Hey, Blanche, it's payday!' I'm tapped out and I could really use the cash.

"Mickey joins in, bellowing from his locker across the room, 'Hey, Johnny, who're they gonna make the check out to—*to whom it may concern?*'

"The date was April 11 and the pay period was ending on April 15, so we would be receiving a short, four-day paycheck to tide us over. My check came to $340 after FICA, Social Security, the New York state and city taxes, and God knows what else.

"When we opened our envelopes, the room went quiet as the guys peered at their paychecks, glancing furtively around the room. Suddenly Mickey's booming voice pierced the silence.

"'Hey, Slick,' he said, 'I thought we were gonna be paid for four days.'

"'Right, Slick,' Whitey replied in an understated, by-the-by manner. (The two of them always referred to each other as Slick.)

" 'Well, shit, Slick,' Mickey shot back, raising his voice, 'How come I only got $10,000?' All Yankees, new and old, fell to the floor laughing.

"You can debate the whole Mickey/Whitey/Duke thing until you're blue in the face, but the truth is that Mickey was the greatest teammate of the three, and for the most part, he was a bigger hero with his teammates than he was with the fans."

---

"It was 1962, and we were playing the Tigers in DEE-troit, as Mickey called it. Yogi and Casey got into a spat in the dugout just before game time, and Casey was really pissed.

" 'Hey, *you*,' he called out to me (he never learned my name—I was either *hey you* or *kid*), 'put on the equipment.'

"It was a blisteringly hot and humid summer day in Detroit, but being a backup catcher, I was excited about getting into the game. I quickly donned my gear and catcher's mask. I guess old Casey and Yogi worked things out, because when the game began, I was on the bench, ready to go, and Yogi is behind the plate after all.

"We get through the second and third innings. Now it's the fourth and I'm sweating bullets, just sitting around on the bench and feeling a tad bit queasy. I get up and stumble over to the ammonia bucket to get a whiff. As I'm bending over the bucket, I happen to glance over my shoulder and see Mickey out in center field, laughing at me. His head and shoulders are rolling and he's having the time of his life.

"Seventh inning, eighth inning, and I still haven't caught a pitch. Each time Mick returns to the dugout, he's laughing so hard that he starts using his hands as blinders so he won't be able to see me, still fully suited up like the Michelin Man and sweating like a pig over the ammonia bucket.

"I never did get into that game, and Casey never did see fit to offer me an explanation. When Casey moved on to coach the Mets, Piggy and Spahnie [Joe Pignatano and

*Mick stretches out a little bit before hitting the cage at Yankee Stadium in 1956.*
Photo courtesy of Lou Requena.

Warren Spahn] told me that one day in the dugout, Casey had shouted, 'Hey, Blanche,' (he had finally learned my name) 'get a bat.'

"'Yo, Skip,' Piggy replied, 'he would, but he's across the river.'"

# BOB TURLEY

**Bullet Bob Turley, who threw his fastball at over 100 miles an hour, spent 8 years with the Yankees in his 12-year career. He was 101–85 and pitched the Yankees to the 1958 World Series title against the Braves with appearances in the last three games. He retired after the 1963 season and made a great deal of money as a financial investor.**

---

"People kid me about the huge salaries pitchers make today and ask me if I would like to be pitching. I tell them I couldn't take the pay cut," Turley said over the phone from his home in Marco Island, Florida.

"I joined the Yankees in 1955 from Baltimore and I could just see how much Mickey loved to play baseball. I don't think I saw anybody with the enthusiasm for the game that Mickey had. One day after we lost to the Brooklyn Dodgers in the Series and went to Japan on an exhibition tour, we almost lost Mickey. People don't know that. Mickey couldn't swim and he got into this pool. It was deeper than he thought, and he suddenly went under. If it wasn't for Whitey [Ford] and Billy [Martin], who were on the edge and jumped in after him and pulled him out, that would have been some end to Mickey's life.

"Mickey was really a cutup and liked to laugh and wanted everybody else on the club to laugh. He used to tell the story of the time when he was a kid player and he struck out and threw the bat from home plate and smashed his helmet. The bat went flying and got into the dugout and broke and crashed against Casey [Stengel]. The Old Man was really pissed. He told Mickey that he had to learn to protect the equipment. The next time up he struck out again. He walked back to the dugout and slowly put his helmet down and put his bat in the rack. Then he walked up to Casey, about six inches from his face, and said, 'Ha, ha, I just struck out.' That broke up everybody on the bench.

"I used to steal signs for Mickey and give him the pitch the opposition pitcher was going to throw. I just picked that skill up from watching these close-ups on television and saw the body movement or how the guy moved his hands. There was one pitcher, Connie Johnson, who pitched for Baltimore, and he had a good screwball. I saw that when he moved to the right on the rubber he would throw the screwball. I told Mickey I knew when Johnson was throwing that tough screwball. 'Let me know.' We made up a whistle signal, and the next day, I saw the guy move and whistled. Mickey hit the ball over the roof. He was the best hitter I ever saw if he knew the pitch and it was in his zone.

"I was living in Baltimore in those days, and I invited all the guys out to my home for a barbecue. I had a big pool, and the guys were having a lot of fun swimming on this off day. Roger Maris began bragging about how great a swimmer he was. Mickey, who couldn't swim a lick, said he would race him the length of the pool. He had made this up ahead of time with Whitey. They both jump in, and Roger is under the water, and Whitey takes a long stick and gives it to Mickey from the edge of the pool, and drags him three-quarters of the way. He floats the rest of the way to the end. The guys pull him out, and suddenly Roger lifts his head from the water and sees Mickey standing on the edge of the pool, screaming, 'I WON, I WON!!!'

"I guess I remember the 1958 Series best, when we came from 3–1 down to beat the Braves. They did it to us the year before. We were on the bus going to the stadium from

*It was never easy out there. Mickey often had to wrap tape around his sore legs—players didn't get much help from trainers in those days.* Photo courtesy of the New York Yankees.

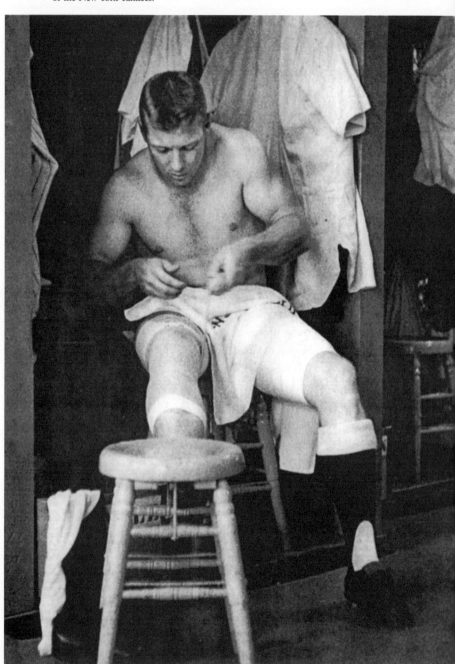

Brown's Lake where we stayed, and it was real quiet before the seventh game. Everybody was thinking about losing two Series in a row. Mickey just stood up in the silent bus and suddenly shouted, 'Is everybody in this bus going to pee in their pants?' That really broke the tension. Everybody started talking and laughing. I relieved [Don] Larsen in the third inning for my third game in a row, shut them down, and we won the game and the Series. With the last out, Mickey just came in and yelled to me, 'You won the Corvette.' That's what they gave the Series MVP.

"I didn't see Mickey much after we got out of the game. I was in business and he was traveling around the country for those autograph shows and golf tournaments. I know he started drinking a lot then, and I know it was just because he was so lonely. He just missed the guys and missed the game. I ran into him at one Old Timers' Game and he just said, 'Gee Pard, I haven't seen you for 10 years. Let's get together some time.' We just never did."

*Mickey hangs out in his favorite booth at his restaurant, where he would meet and greet well-wishers, sign autographs, and generally hold court.* Photo courtesy of Bill Liederman.

# Mantle as Personality

## BILL LIEDERMAN

**Bill Liederman was a championship high school tennis player and an outstanding college basketball player who settled for softball in Central Park after his dream of playing for the Yankees ended in a blaze of glory. He was the founder of a New York restaurant school. When he sold the school, he decided to open a sports restaurant. All he needed was a good location and a prominent partner. He approached Mickey Mantle, who agreed to participate in the deal after Liederman told him the new place would be another Toots Shor's, a hangout for sports fans, athletes, and young businesspeople. The restaurant opened in 1988.**

---

"Mickey always had a very healthy distrust for Yankees owner George Steinbrenner. In Mickey's mind, George wasn't a baseball guy. He came from Cleveland, and Mickey hated Cleveland. Mick was also furious that George had fired his pal Yogi Berra just 16 games into the 1985 season. Most of all,

Mickey felt George was a shady businessman seeking to pawn off the great Yankees tradition, which the Mick himself had helped to build. He would bristle when George's name came up, making his signature farting noise from the side of his mouth.

"One afternoon, as Mickey was holding court at his usual table, listening to Patsy Cline and watching blooper tapes, George burst through the revolving doors, flanked by beefy security guards swathed in ill-fitting dark suits. Mick acknowledged George and beckoned him toward the table as if he were calling for a right-hander out of the bullpen. With a flip of his wrist, George dismissed his muscle and took the seat across from Mickey. The air was thick with tension, so I excused myself from the table and took my post a few feet away. In the battle of charismatic icons, Mick was the heavy favorite, and George began to sink into the booth.

"Their increasingly heated discussion centered on the use of the stadium in Fort Lauderdale for Mickey's fantasy baseball camp. Although the field (which at that time was still the official spring-training site of the Yankees) was owned by the city of Fort Lauderdale, George had the right of approval on who could use it. Campers donned authentic Yankees uniforms, which implied an official association with the Yankees team. As George and Mickey bickered about the field, the uniforms, and Mick's much-mentioned preference not to attend Old Timers' Games (he was shy in public and just didn't want the attention), Mickey grew cross, jammed his tongue into the side of his cheek, and started to measure his adversary for the kill. As Mickey outnegotiated George at every turn, a deal began to emerge: Mickey could continue to hold fantasy camps in Fort Lauderdale and use the Yankees pinstripes for his campers' duds in exchange for one more appearance at Old Timers' Day.

"George wanted the uniforms and playing field to be contingent upon Mick's guaranteed annual appearance. Old Timers' Day had always meant a lot to George, and he monitored it closely, with particular attention to who was invited and the order in which his honored Yankees guests were to be introduced onto the field. With Yogi already boycotting the event and Joe D. hitting George up for an appearance fee to the tune of $50,000 a year, losing Mick would just add insult to injury. Despite his money, his world titles in '77 and '78, his popular appeal, and his infamy, George would never break into the exclusive club of good-old-boy ex-Yankees legends.

"Mickey had a poker face fit for the World Series of Poker, and he held his ground, his laser stare searing into Steinbrenner's head, heart, and soul.

"'C'mon, Mickey,' he whined, 'as long as you show up for Old Timers' Day you can use the field.'

"'F*** you, George,' Mickey drawled, 'and get the hell out of my restaurant.'

"George sat there in silence, as though shot with a stun gun. After a pregnant pause, George finally got up and scampered out of the restaurant with his tail between his legs, stripped of his usual peacock strut. As soon as he was out of earshot, Mick replaced his grimace with his trademark thousand-watt smile and roared with laughter, most impressed at his own knack for practical joking."

---

"Mickey and I were taking simultaneous dumps about three thousand miles apart—I was in Manhattan and he was in Dallas—when he made his usual early morning call to me. I was reading the *New York Post* when the phone rang, and I picked up the bathroom extension, which was conveniently located within arm's length of the throne. Mickey offered his usual greeting:

"'Hey, Pard,' he drawled 'I'm taking a shit and I was thinking about you.'

"'How unusual,' I replied, thumbing through the newspaper. He always began our phone conversations that way.

"'My sons need something to do,' he continued. 'They want to open a Mickey Mantle's Restaurant.'

"'Oh, in Dallas? That's great,' I replied, 'I'd be happy to help . . .'

"'Nah,' he interrupted, 'we won't be needing your help. And by the way, you can take my name off your restaurant.'

"The *Post* slipped from my hands to the tile floor, and I began to hyperventilate as visions of bankruptcy danced in my head. The restaurant had been open for about five years, and things were finally starting to come together for me financially.

"'I only want my name on one restaurant, and I think *my* boys should own it,' Mickey explained with casual abandon.

"'But . . . M-Mickey,' I stammered, 'We have a *contract*.'

"'F*** the contract,' he spat, 'Just come up with another name, like Bill Liederman's Sports Bar, maybe.'

"'Mickey, I'm beggin' ya,' I whimpered, 'I just spent the last five years of my life building the place up from the ground. And besides, I'm just a regular guy. My name wouldn't work.'

"'Why not, Pard? Everyone knows you up there in New York.' A dead silence ensued as I opened and closed my mouth several times, trying to craft a winning rebuttal. Looking to buy time, I finally suggested that Mickey's three sons intern at my place for six months in order to get a feel for the operation. I figured that would be sufficient time for them to learn to hate the restaurant business.

"'Nah,' Mickey mused, 'I want them to train with some *real* pros down here in Dallas.'

"I gritted my teeth. 'OK, Mick,' I began, 'what's your time frame on this?' I was a dead man talking.

"'I'll give you until Monday to take my name down,' he offered. It was Friday.

"We both sat there in silence, meditating on the matter at hand and taking care of our respective bathroom functions. I glanced at the *New York Post* at my feet, and in so doing, I happened to notice the date inscribed on the masthead: April 1, 1993.

"'April Fools', Pard,' Mickey chirped, and promptly hung up, eager to ring his next victim.

P.S.: April first was Mickey's favorite national holiday. Each year, he would ring in the fourth month by calling Whitey, Yogi, and his kids in turn, torturing them with his follies. Most amusing, Pard.

———————————

"A cranky and very testy Mickey was parked at a long, banquet-style table with his coaching staff for the fantasy camp: Moose Skowron, Hank Bauer, Ron Guidry, Jake Gibbs, Johnny Blanchard, and Catfish Hunter, among others. The occasion was a fantasy-camp reunion at the restaurant for campers and their families. Wanda Greer, the camp administrator, had decided to allow two autographs per guest from each ex-Yankee, a choice she and I would live to regret. I watched in horror as what should have been a quaint little back-slapping old-pals reunion spiraled into a freakish autograph show as fantasy campers and friends pushed and shoved to get in line for Mickey's signature, ignoring the other players. As dozens of frenzied fans swarmed about him, the situation turned awkward. The idea had been for fans to collect autographs from all the ex-Yankees at the table, not just from Mickey. As Mickey sensed his cronies' discomfort, his temperature started to rise. He soon reached the boiling point as guests tried to filibuster their way into just one more autograph for their 'dying twin brother.'

"The next person in line was a teenage boy, clad in hip-hop-style baggy jeans and Starter jacket. As Mickey looked up from his last autograph and caught a glimpse of the youth, he recoiled.

"'Wait a second,' he hissed. 'Are you a f***ing dealer?' I had to spend several minutes assuring Mickey that the shell-shocked teen was the son of a fantasy camper and *not* a memorabilia dealer before he grudgingly signed the young man's baseball."

"Mickey was spending a leisurely afternoon at booth number 32 in the restaurant, sipping white-wine spritzers and engaging in the business of being Mickey Mantle. As was my custom whenever Mick dined alone, I dropped everything I was doing to sit across the booth from him, negotiating/officiating autograph requests and sliding over to allow certain fans an audience when Mick gestured subtly at me to signal his approval.

"At one point, Rocky Bleier, a Vietnam War hero and a member of the four-time Super Bowl champion Pittsburgh Steelers, approached our table. With a look of utmost respect and recognition, Mickey motioned for Rocky to be seated. Just then, I received an urgent phone call from Vice President Dan Quayle's office.

"'This is So-and-So, the advance person for Vice President Quayle,' a female voice roared through the phone. 'The vice president is holding a press conference at the Plaza Hotel and would like to stop over and say hello to Mickey.'

"'I'll ask him,' I replied, uncertain as to how Mickey might respond.

"'OK, just one thing,' the advance person warned. '*Please* keep this under your hat. The vice president doesn't want the press to catch wind of his visit with Mickey.'

"'Hey Mick,' I stammered, trying to downplay my excitement at this potential public-relations bonanza, 'Vice P-President Quayle is at the P-Plaza and he wants to come by and meet you. Is that OK?'

"'I don't give a f***,' he declared. 'You decide.'

"I gave Ms. Advance Lady the good news, and she reminded me once again to be discreet about the rendezvous.

"Meanwhile, back at the Plaza, Quayle was concluding his speech to the throngs of press at the conference. His final remarks were as follows: 'I'm going up the street to see Mickey Mantle at his restaurant!'

*Mick is flanked by then–Vice President Dan Quayle (right) and a secret service agent.* Photo courtesy of Bill Liederman.

"Smelling a story, the gaggle of eager reporters played fol-low the leader and tore down the street after Quayle with about a dozen TV cameras in tow. Moments later, the veep exploded into the restaurant with reckless abandon, flanked by a posse of press, staffers, and Secret Service detail.

"As Quayle approached our table, Mickey and Rocky Bleier stood up to offer their greetings.

"'Mickey,' Quayle's mouthpiece declared pompously, 'this is the vice president of the United States, Dan Quayle.'

"Suppressing an I-don't-give-a-shit type of reaction, Mickey responded in turn by introducing Rocky Bleier to the man just one heartbeat away from the most powerful leader of the free world.

"'Why Rocky,' said the veep, "didn't you play with Mickey on the Yankees?'

"Despite the fact that the 20-year age differential would have made this chronologically impossible, the thing that really shocked Mickey was Quayle's failure to recognize Bleier, an American icon in his own right. Mick shot one of his patented you're-a-dumb-shit looks at the VP.

"'No, Mr. Vice President,' Bleier responded, 'I played football for the Steelers.'

"'Oh, I didn't know you played in the National League,' said Mr. Potato*e* Head.

"Embarrassed that his guest had been dissed, Mickey turned away from Quayle and resumed his conversation with Rocky as the cast of thousands drained from the restaurant."

---

"*Sports Illustrated* swimsuit model and pro volleyball sen-sation Gabrielle Reece was holding a press event at Mantle's to promote the pro volleyball tour. Mickey was dining in the restaurant that day and had had his arm twisted by a PR dweeb about posing with Reece for some pictures. At 6'3" of sculpted athletic femininity, she towered over Mickey in all her glory when they posed together for the shutterbugs. As

Mickey cuddled up next to her for the photo, his libido sprang into action.

"'Hey baby,' he whispered, 'let's get together for a drink later.'

"'Mr. Mantle,' Gabrielle inquired with disdain, 'is that the way you'd talk to your granddaughter?'"

---

"A large auction house was holding a press event at the restaurant to promote an auction featuring a game-worn Mickey Mantle jersey. Mick had been retained by the auction company to appear at the press conference and pimp the sale of the jersey and other game-used Mickey paraphernalia. As he stood at the podium holding his coveted jersey, a reporter asked the auctioneer how much it might fetch in the sale. 'Between seventy-five and a hundred thousand dollars,' he replied.

"Up until this point, Mick had been sort of snoozing through the event, but now he bolted upright at the mention of the astronomical figure. He loosened his belt, dropped his pants, and asked, 'Anyone wanna buy my shorts?'

"Many hands shot up in the audience as Mickey pulled his pants back up and sauntered toward the exit with a big, wide, country-boy grin on his impish face."

---

"It was opening night at Mantle's, February 13, 1988. The event had been highly anticipated, and everyone and their mother were scrounging for admission. Dozens of A-list celebrities were in attendance that night, and I was thrilled to see Yogi Berra, Whitey Ford, Phil Rizzuto, Billy Martin, Howard Cosell, Peter Jennings, George Steinbrenner, Frank Gifford, Sylvester Stallone, and Don Johnson jammed in like tuxedo-clad sardines with about five or six hundred other well-wishers. The restaurant was filled to at least double its capacity.

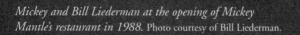

*Mickey and Bill Liederman at the opening of Mickey Mantle's restaurant in 1988.* Photo courtesy of Bill Liederman.

"Mickey and his Yankees buddies were cloistered in the back room. My eight-year-old daughter, Chloe, was with me that evening, and I struggled to baby-sit and host the event all at once. People were literally fighting to get in the door. It was anarchy. At one point, I turned around and Chloe was nowhere to be seen. I fought my way through the teeming throng to the rear of the restaurant, frantically scanning the area for any sign of my kid.

"'Daddy,' I heard her wail. 'Where's my daddy?' I pushed my way in the direction of the childish wails and saw Chloe perched in Billy Martin's lap. Mickey was next to them speaking sweetly to my tearful daughter. 'Don't worry, Babe,' he assured her. 'You're sitting on the lap of the manager of the New York Yankees!'

"Chloe's face lit up as I caught her eye and approached the table.

"'Don't worry, Pard,' said the Mick, 'We'll take care of her.'"

---

"I had a highlighted section on the menu called 'Mickey's Favorites.' The items included chicken-fried steak, chicken potpie, and sirloin chili. Another item I stuck in, without checking with Mickey, was lobster ravioli, a tasty dish that seemed fit for this special category.

"A young customer, about 13, with a strong New York accent and a city smirk, asked with adolescent sarcasm, 'Is lobster ravioli really one of your favorites?'

"Although Mickey never lost his temper with me, he could get testy and possessed the Look, an emotionally crippling stare. Mickey, milking the moment, looked at the menu, peered up at me with a blank stare, turned slowly to the youngster, gestured with his finger for the kid to move in closer, and said firmly, 'Kid, I grew up on that stuff.'"

---

"Mickey Mantle was eating at his usual table one evening when his dining companion popped a Valium. Mickey wasn't drinking at that time, and he said, 'Hey, let me try one of those.' Twenty minutes later, a relaxed and particularly easy-going Mick was going from patron to patron at the bar, grinning with all of his might, saying, 'Hi, I'm Mickey Mantle. Do you want my autograph?'"

---

"In the early days of the restaurant, Mickey came in one morning at around 8:00 A.M. to shoot an A&W Root Beer commercial. Billing himself as "One-Take Mickey" and working on almost no sleep, he proceeded to do the commercial in exactly one take and headed out of the restaurant hours before it would open to lunchtime customers. At that very moment, two tourists were attempting to gain entrance in order to buy T-shirts. Mick and the tourists collided in the doorway. 'I can't believe it,' one tourist exclaimed. 'It's Mickey Mantle!' Mickey was taken off guard and responded, 'Go f*** yourself!' The tourist then turned to his wife and said, with boundless glee, 'I can't believe Mickey Mantle just told me to go f*** myself!' A contrite Mickey immediately apologized, signed autographs, and invited them back later for lunch on him."

---

"Mickey and Billy Martin were having lunch in the rear of the restaurant. Hearing that they were in the house, a local TV station sent Warner Wolf over with his camera crew to interview the two of them. Unbeknownst to Mickey and Billy, Warner had recently survived open-heart surgery. Mickey and Billy both got down on all fours and hid behind a nearby column. When Warner came looking for them, they leaped out from behind the column growling like rabid dogs, latching onto Warner's pant legs with their teeth. Warner almost had a heart attack while Mick and Billy watched, rolling on the floor with laughter."

―――――――――――

"Mickey was always very protective of and loyal to the restaurant employees. One of our female bartenders was being stalked by a psycho customer and Mickey got word of it. The next time Mickey came in, the stalker was standing outside, harassing the barkeep with lewd gestures. Mick dragged the offender into the restaurant and ushered him through the dining room to the courtyard out back. Mickey shoved the guy against the wall, put his finger in his face, and said, 'Son, the next time you bother one of my girls I'm going to take you back out here and give you a good ass-whipping.' We never saw the guy again."

―――――――――――

"Mickey was constantly hounded for autographs no matter where he went. At the restaurant, fans would actually follow him into the men's room to pester him. Often I would escort him to the bathroom in order to help ensure his privacy and to avoid incident.

"On one such occasion, Mickey was in the process of doing number one when a crazed fan snuck up behind him and tapped him on the shoulder.

" 'Mr. Mantle, I'm your biggest fan,' he said. 'Can I have your autograph?'

"Stunned, Mickey whirled around to his left and peed all over the young man's slacks. 'Why would you ask me for an autograph while I'm taking a piss?' "

―――――――――――

"Mickey insisted that all our servers wear nametags so that he could call them by name. The nametags were clipped onto the uniform, just above the left breast. On occasion, after holding court in the restaurant for several hours, Mickey would ask female servers, 'If that one's named Amy, what's the other one called?' "

*Mickey in his favorite western garb. After all, the guy was from Oklahoma, lived in Texas, and never called the Bronx his home—just his place of business.* Photo courtesy of the Mantle family.

---

"Mickey invited me and about a half-dozen other friends to dinner to celebrate his birthday. For the venue, he selected Tse Yang, a posh Chinese restaurant on the Upper East Side. When we arrived, the maître d' ushered us back to a private room reserved for VIP guests. When the waiter appeared at the table, Mick ordered 'a few bottles of that red shit.' Little did Mickey know, 'that red shit' was actually a Mondavi Opus, which goes for about $195 a bottle. As it was his birthday celebration, the group consumed six bottles of 'that red shit.' Along with the food, the bill came to $1,875. When Mick laid eyes on the check, he frowned at the waiter and said, 'Sheeeeet, nineteen hundred dollars is a lot of money for Chinese food.'"

---

"Mickey didn't like to make appearances. He didn't like to be in the spotlight, and he didn't need the money. Once, I got a call from some guy wanting to know if he could hire Mickey to appear at his son's bar mitzvah. Mickey was in his usual booth at the time, so I asked him.

"'Hey, Mick,' I proffered. 'How much for an appearance at a bar mitzvah?'

"'F*** bar mitzvahs,' he drawled, the Hebrew words dribbling awkwardly from his Okie, country-boy lips (I don't even think Mickey knew what a bar mitzvah was for). 'Tell 'em fifty grand,' he instructed, expecting to blow the man off with his astronomical price tag.

"So I tell the bar mitzvah boy's daddy, and he said, 'Deal!' as though fifty Gs was the bargain of the century.

"P.S.: Mickey made the appearance and had a good time at the party."

---

"Mickey made a lot of appearances at guys' big four-oh parties. He made one once at a major rag-trader's over-the-hill birthday bash. The birthday boy's wife drew up a table chart that, for some reason, had Mickey and the guest of honor at adjacent tables. Mickey was getting bored, and he began pounding his Tanqueray and tonics. All of a sudden, the Mick grabbed a dinner roll from the bread basket, wound up, and pegged it at the birthday boy's head. The bun hurtled through the air at about a hundred miles per hour and landed right on the money, just north of the guy's right ear, exploding in a halo of dough around his shiny, bald pate.

"The guest of honor took a moment to pick some crust out of his eye and then retaliated by lobbing an onion ring, a Texas-league blooper that landed squarely on the jacket zipper of Mickey's brand-new velour sweat suit. For Mick, it was now Game 7 of the food-fighting World Series, and he was ready to play. He picked the greasy morsel off his chest and began fighting from both sides of the plate, pelting his foe with both hands. *Bam*: a barbecued rib hit him on the shoulder. *Doink*: chicken-fried steak to the midsection. *Boing*: a butter patty to the chin. *Rat-tat-tat-tat*: ratatouille. *Splash*: Tanqueray and tonic everywhere.

Soon the birthday boy was buried in victuals and managed a final mashed-potato grenade before surrendering. Rising from his seat, he waved a gravy-splooged napkin and approached Mickey, wearing his new birthday suit: Mickey's entire dinner.

" 'Happy birthday, Pard,' Mickey offered, giving the birthday boy a big, dirty bear hug.

"The birthday boy turned to his horrified wife and said, 'Honey, it just doesn't get any better than this!' "

---

"In 1988, Mickey was providing color commentary on Yankees games for Cablevision, and shortly after the restaurant opened, he had Whitey Ford on as a guest in the broadcast booth during the show. In between pitches, Whitey asked, 'So Mick, how's the steak in your new restaurant?'

"Mickey bent over and took off one of his black loafers and jammed it directly into his mouth as he cried, 'Tastes like shoe leather!'

"The next day, I summoned up enough courage to mention the faux pas to my childhood idol/brand-new business partner. 'Mickey,' I cooed, 'it's probably not a great idea to liken our steaks to shoe leather.'

"There was a long moment as he held me in his fearsome gaze.

" 'OK, Pard,' he said finally."

---

"Shortly after the opening of Mantle's in 1988, Regis Philbin invited Mickey and our chef, Randy Pietro, on his show to demonstrate how to make chicken-fried steak. Before we got in the limo with Randy, Mickey asked me, 'What's our chef's name?' 'Randy,' I told him.

"Once we were at the studio, on our way to the set, Mick asked again, 'What's the name of our chef?'

"'It's *Randy*,' I repeated.

"Moments later Mickey was on the air, live with Regis and Chef Randy. 'What's your chef's name, Mick?' Regis inquired as the interview began.

"A pregnant pause ensued, and after several moments of uncomfortable silence, Mick replied, 'We just call him Chef.'

"On the return limo ride, Mickey gave me one of those legendary Mickey-hairy-eyeball looks and said, 'Damn, Bill. Why didn't you tell me the chef's name beforehand?' "

---

"Mickey brought me down to Florida every fall to be the 'permanent catcher' at his fantasy baseball camp in Fort Lauderdale, the former spring-training home of the Yankees during Mickey's glory days. The camp's staff, or coaches, comprised a glittering list of former Yankees greats. In addition to schmoozing with their childhood heroes, the campers played a doubleheader every day, and the week climaxed with a fantasy game of campers versus the former Yankees icons. Because the average age of the campers was near-deceased, Mickey couldn't get them to strap on the tools of ignorance and squat for hours in the broiling Florida sun. Furthermore, a camper-catcher would have slowed the game down to a crawl in a hailstorm of passed balls and wild tosses back to the pitcher. I had always been a catcher, and it was easy for me to crouch behind the plate and toss the ball back to Whitey, Goose, Guidry, or whoever was on the mound. Catching high pop fouls behind the plate, however, proved to be far more difficult.

Mickey traveled from field to field on a golf cart, calling out instructions and verbally abusing campers and coaches alike. "I flubbed a few easy pop-ups behind the dish and turned around to see Mickey shaking his head as if to say, 'You're horseshit.' He pulled me aside after the inning to chew out my ass.

"'As a catcher, your defense reminds me of Yogi's,' he remarked. [Yogi was not known for his defensive skill.] 'You gotta get those pop-ups,' he continued. 'You're f***ing up the game.'

"'I'll tell you what,' he went on. 'Every time you catch one, I'll give you a hundred bucks. Every time you miss, you give *me* a hundred bucks. How 'bout that?' I didn't feel like I had a choice, so I agreed.

"'And don't be thinking just because I'm at another field, I won't know about it,' he warned, wagging his finger at me as he zoomed away in his little white cart.

"Flash forward to the next several innings, during which I really started to f*** up. All the campers and coaches were counting as I was into Mickey for four, five, and six hundred

*Mickey and Liederman, restaurateur and fantasy camp backstop.*
Photo courtesy of Bill Liederman.

dollars. I went to Johnny Blanchard and begged him for a few pointers.

"'Blanche,' I asked him as another pop foul dropped to the dirt at my feet, 'what am I doing wrong?'

"'Bill,' he explained, 'when you get under the ball, you're hopping back and forth on your feet. So you're probably seeing two or three balls up there instead of just one.'

"He was right. I was.

"'When you get under the ball,' Blanche said, 'you gotta plant your feet, and don't put your mitt over your eyes. That oughta help.'

"It did help, and little by little, I began to catch up to Mickey on the ledger sheet. On the last day of camp, the campers played the Yankees legends, and because Blanchard and Gibbs weren't about to get down on their knees behind the plate, I was ordained the starting catcher for the New York Yankees. Here's the lineup:

> *Rivers CF*
> *Kubek SS*
> *Boyer 3B*
> *Skowron 1B*
> *Richardson 2B*
> *Whitaker RF*
> *Murcer LF*
> *Guidry P*
> *Liederman C*

"Not bad. The stands were packed with friends and family, campers, and the usual collection of brain-dead autograph hounds. I was behind the plate, trying to catch Guidry's 90-mile-per-hour sliders, thinking *focus, focus, focus*. Of course, the first batter for the campers' team hit a high fly ball directly behind home plate—an easy play to make, if you know how.

Mickey was coaching at first base, and he jogged down the first-base line and stood next to me, directly beneath the descending ball.

"'Miss, *miss*, MISS,' he screamed, for the benefit of the entire crowd. I obliged him by missing and tripping over his feet in the process, falling flat on my face.

"'That's another hundred,' he pronounced, and sauntered back to first base.

"Two innings later, it was my turn at bat. Bear in mind that I hadn't picked up a bat all week, and now I was in the batter's box with Mickey standing right beside me. The bases were drunk with Yankees: Rivers, Moose, and Richardson.

"'Bill,' Mickey said, 'you owe me seven hundred dollars. Tell you what: let's go double or nothing on a home run.'

"No sooner did I nod my approval of this new arrangement than the loudspeaker blared, 'Now batting for the Yankees, No. 42, Bill Liederman. He runs Mickey's restaurant in New York. Let's see if he can hit like his boss.'

"I dug into the batter's box. The first pitch was down the middle, and I swung, lifting a high fly ball out to deep center field. I thought it was going out, but Mickey knew better. 'Warning-track power, just like Murcer,' he bellowed as the ball was caught 20 feet from the wall.

"I was deflated, and now I was out fourteen hundred bucks, but feeling almost like a real baseball player. I tried to pay off my debt on many occasions, but Mickey never let me."

## CHARLEY DANIELS

**This legendary country musician is a three-time Grammy winner and has received six platinum records. His ditty "The Devil Went Down to Georgia" was Mickey's favorite.**

"In August of 1989, I was doing a gig at Yankee Stadium. Mickey came to the concert unannounced and incognito with a huge bull-rider's hat pulled all the way down to his ears. He looked like the village idiot. After the show he surprised me backstage, and instead of hobnobbing with the other celebs, he insisted on shaking hands with every member of the road and grounds crew. After the concert, Mickey called me and left a message concerning lyrics in a new song: *What the world needs now is a few more rednecks like John Wayne and Mickey Mantle.*

"'Hey Charley,' Mickey said, 'I love your new song, but did you have to include John Wayne?'"

## DICK FOX

**This former William Morris agent is credited with having launched the careers of Billy Crystal and Eddie Murphy. His clients include Jerry Lewis, Frankie Avalon, Fabian, and Bobbie Rydell.**

———————————

"In 1988 I attended Mickey Mantle's fantasy baseball camp, as a birthday gift from my wife and son. I donned the pinstripes with No. 7 emblazoned on the back and proceeded to commit countless errors, strike out repeatedly, and get treated for myriad injuries to my hands, feet, hamstring, and groin. I ended up on the DL for the last game of the week. Mickey plunked himself down next to me in the dugout, turned to me with a look of total disgust, and uttered, 'Fox, you're the worst f***ing teammate I've had in my entire life.'"

## SPENCER ROSS

**A close friend of Mickey's, this radio personality has served as the voice of the Jets, Yankees, and Nets and is currently the voice of the Knicks and Rangers.**

*A mutual admiration society: Mickey and Charley Daniels at a Yankee Stadium concert in 1989.*
Photo courtesy of Tom Molito.

"In 1986, I decided to open a sports apparel store—no memorabilia, all the name brands of athletic shoes, sweat suits, socks, and T-shirts. I called it Spencer Ross' Clubhouse, and many local athletes visited and spent hours signing autographs for nothing more than a thank-you—Billy Martin, Whitey Ford, Phil Rizzuto, Lou Piniella, and Phil Simms, to name a few. Then one day there was Mickey approaching me with a serious look on his face. I could tell something was bothering him. 'Spence,' he began, 'are you mad at me?'

"'No, Mick, of course not,' I told him. 'Why would I be mad at you?'

"He kind of smiled and said, 'Well, I know you opened up that store in New Jersey. I know you've had Whitey, Billy, and Scooter come over and sign autographs. I figured you might be mad at me and that's why you haven't asked me to make an appearance.'

"I considered Mick a friend, but I also knew that signing autographs was his livelihood, and remember, we're talking about a man who earned millions of dollars each year simply by signing his name. His time was a precious commodity.

"'No, Mick, I'm not mad at you. I just thought you might not have the time.'

"Mickey smiled his big smile and said, 'Well, let's *find* the time.'

"And he did. The crowds were lined around the block for three hours at the shop in Glen Rock, New Jersey, as Mick sat there smiling and signing autographs. After the appearance, he insisted on taking my family and me to the finest restaurant in the area. En route he let me know, 'This one's on me. You try and pick up that check, I'll break your arm.' Of course I knew he was kidding, but I kept my hand in my pocket when the bill came around."

# LAWRENCE MELI

**As president of the Goodlife TV Network, and as a broad-casting executive with the Sports Channel, Lawrence Meli hired Mickey to appear as a color commentator of Yankees games during the mid- to late eighties.**

---

"My family was touched by the challenges of raising hearing-impaired sons. Mickey had met my two oldest, Peter and John, and was truly moved by their plight. One night, as we finished a Yankees-Angels game, Mickey asked if he could do anything to help the boys. I responded by asking Mickey if he would accompany me to Washington, D.C., to visit certain congressmen and senators who could be very influential in funding research for the causes of and cures for deafness.

"Flying anywhere with Mickey was always great fun, but flying to Washington and hearing Mick recollect his last visit there [as a player] was intriguing. Mick talked about how he loved to play the Washington Senators and how President Eisenhower always brought him good luck on Opening Day as Mickey drove yet another one out of the stadium.

"We arrived at Capitol Hill, and for anyone who's never seen it, it looks like hundreds of stairs. Mick climbed them in noticeable discomfort and proceeded to greet a half-dozen senators and congressmen. 'My friend here has some hearing-impaired sons and I want to help them,' he said.

"'We're here to ask you to support the creation of a National Institute on Deafness as part of the National Institutes of Health,' I added.

"After our visits were complete and Mick had signed countless autographs [he often said to me, 'By this time, everyone in America must have my autograph'] he looked at me and said, 'So this is lobbying, huh?' I answered that indeed it was, and with a twinkle in his eye he said, 'Don't ever want to do *that* again.'

"In 1989, one of the last official acts of President Ronald Reagan was to ratify the creation of the National Institute of Deafness and Other Communicative Disorders."

## BARRY HALPER

**A part-owner of the New York Yankees, Barry Halper is widely recognized as the world's greatest collector of baseball memorabilia. His artifacts are on display in his wing of Cooperstown's Hall of Fame.**

---

"I happened to be in Dallas on business on August 9, 1995—the day when Mickey held a press conference at Baylor University Hospital with Dr. Robert Goldstein after he had recovered from his liver-replacement surgery. I sat in the back of the room and listened as Mickey discussed his condition in a weak voice. He advised his fans to take care of their bodies and not to be like him.

"After his remarks, he noticed me in the back of the room. 'Hey, Barry, do you want my old liver? I know you have Ty Cobb's teeth.'

"'No,' I replied. 'But how about the scalpel from the operation?' Everybody laughed ghoulishly. Four days later I received a FedEx package from Baylor Hospital from Mickey and the surgeon. Enclosed I found a funky-smelling, white, latex glove with two brown-tipped fingers along with a handwritten note from Mickey. 'Barry,' it read, 'this is the glove from my hemorrhoid exam. Best wishes, Mickey Mantle.'"

## DAVID HALBERSTAM

**David Halberstam, a Pulitzer Prize–winning author and reporter, has written many books on baseball, including**

*The Teammates,* the study of the friendship of four members of the Boston Red Sox—Ted Williams, Dom DiMaggio, Bobby Doerr, and Johnny Pesky.

———————

"I remember when Mickey told me the story of having a long night and coming to Yankee Stadium without any sleep and then having to go right into the game. 'If they knew how hard this was they wouldn't bother me so much.' Mickey was certainly unique."

## BERT RANDOLPH SUGAR

**Bert Sugar is a writer, historian, lecturer, and bon vivant with an expertise in boxing second to none. He is a familiar sight on television interview programs about boxing with the large fedora on his head and the unlit cigar dangling from his lips. He spent a lot of happy hours with Mickey at New York restaurants and nightspots, especially after high-profile boxing matches.**

———————

"Mickey told me about the time he was out with Billy Martin when Billy was visiting him during the off-season at his Dallas home. Mickey and Billy stayed out real late together, and when Mickey arrived home just before daybreak he took his shoes off, snuck into the house to avoid wife Merlyn's wrath for the outing, and sat gingerly on the bed.

"He began removing his socks when Merlyn suddenly woke up.

"'Where are you going?' she asked.

"'Just going fishing with Billy,' Mickey quickly replied.

"He got up, went back downstairs with his shoes and socks in his hand, put them on at the bottom step, and left the house."

## ROY WHITE

**Roy White played 15 years with the Yankees, from 1965 through 1979. He batted .271 with 160 career home runs. He played on three Yankee pennant winners, in 1976, 1977, and 1978, and two world championship teams. He then played three more seasons in Japan. He is the only man in history to bat fourth behind both Mickey Mantle and Sadaharu Oh, the great Japanese home-run slugger. White worked in the Yankees' front office, later coached in the minor leagues for the Oakland A's, and was named the first-base coach of the Yankees for the 2004 season.**

---

"I went to Japan after the 1979 season because I still thought I had some baseball left in me. I had done everything in U.S. baseball: played on three pennant winners and two Series champions, played in the All-Star Game, and played with those great Yankees like Mickey, Whitey Ford, Elston Howard, and the rest. I really enjoyed my time in Japan. It was a wonderful experience.

"I batted fourth behind Sadaharu Oh for a while. That was exciting. He was a great hitter. I don't think he would have been a great home-run guy here in the U.S., but he was a wonderful hitter and would have had a high average here. He really knew about hitting. The Japanese don't have many left-handed pitchers, so that was an advantage for him. When I batted fourth behind him, I recalled that I had batted fourth behind Mickey in a few games. That was something. Sadaharu Oh was a tremendous home-run hitter in Japan, where the parks are smaller and the pitchers don't throw as hard as they do here. But he was no Mickey Mantle. Nobody was. Mickey was the only guy with that kind of power from both sides of the plate. There was only one Mickey. Nobody really could match him. I was a switch-hitter, and hit a few home runs, but mine just snuck into the seats. Mickey's homers always

*Merlyn Mantle and her four sons: (front) Bill and Mickey Jr. and (back) David and Danny.* Photo courtesy of AP/Wide World Photos.

were high and far and looked like they might make it out
of the stadium. Nobody ever did that like him. It was a thrill
to play those few years with Mickey. He wasn't at his best
when I joined the team. I still think he was pretty good.
I couldn't help but think about what Mickey must have
been like when he was young, and how far he could hit a
baseball.

"I would have enjoying watching Sadaharu Oh playing
here. I enjoyed watching Mickey play here. There were always
two levels in baseball: there was Mickey, and then there were
the rest of us."

## BOBBY VALENTINE

**Bobby Valentine spent 10 years in the big leagues as a
player but made his baseball name as a controversial manager. He made it to the World Series with the New York
Mets in 2000 and was fired after the 2002 season. He is
now managing in Japan for his second time.**

---

"I had been a big star in high school in Connecticut. I
was invited to Yankee Stadium by Mike Burke who ran the
team for CBS. He took me into the clubhouse and introduced
me to some of the players. I got to meet Mickey Mantle. I was
so nervous I thought I would faint. Mickey looked at me and
said, 'Want my job, kid?' Then he just started giggling."

## ARTHUR RICHMAN

**Arthur Richman has been around baseball nearly 70 years
as a young fan of Babe Ruth and Lou Gehrig in the Bronx,
a sportswriter, and then a baseball executive. He is now an
assistant to Yankees owner George Steinbrenner.**

"When I was promotions director of the Mets we had a day with all the great New York center fielders, Joe DiMaggio, Willie Mays, Duke Snider, and Mickey Mantle. They were tough to take care of before the event except for Mantle. I just gave Mickey a bottle of vodka. He just sat there and sipped it out of a paper cup. He was smiling and telling jokes to the other players all the time."

## JEROME HOLTZMAN

**Jerome Holtzman is Major League Baseball's official historian after a brilliant Hall of Fame career as a sportswriter for the *Chicago Sun-Times* and the *Chicago Tribune*.**

"I was chairman of the Chicago baseball writers in the winter of 1965. We arranged for Sandy Koufax and Mickey Mantle to come to our dinner. A company called me up and gave me a limousine to use to pick up the players. I drove out to O'Hare Airport and picked up Mantle. He was great. On the way in to his hotel I asked him if he would be willing to detour a few minutes to visit with my kids in my home in Evanston. They were too young to come to the dinner, and they looked on him as such a great hero. He said he would be happy to do it. He came into the house, played with the kids, signed their autograph books, and spent 45 minutes there like a member of our family. He has always been a hero of mine for that."

## DICK LYNCH

**Dick Lynch was a defensive back for the New York Football Giants from 1959 to 1966. He later became a**

broadcaster. He lost a son, Richard Jr., at the World Trade Center on September 11, 2001.

---

"We played in Yankee Stadium in those days, and I would run into Mickey often. He was just a fun guy to be around. He bragged about his football skills in school, and I bragged about my baseball skills at Notre Dame. We were both lying. We had a few hangouts where the athletes would meet. When Mickey came in it was very special. He was quick at putting down his money and buying rounds. I know all that stuff about thinking he would die early because so many in his family had. He sure lived hard, but he had fun. Isn't that what it's all about?"

## BUCK SHOWALTER

**William Nathaniel "Buck" Showalter, the manager of the Texas Rangers, began his managerial career with the New York Yankees. He brought them to the playoffs against Seattle in 1995. He later became the manager of the Arizona Diamondbacks and now the Texas Rangers. Both the Yankees and the Diamondbacks, teams that Showalter built, won the World Series shortly after he left them.**

---

Buck Showalter was introduced to Mickey Mantle at Mickey Mantle's restaurant, across from Central Park in Manhattan, shortly after Showalter became manager of the Yankees. "Hi, Bucky, nice to meet you," Mickey said.

"Thanks, Mickey. Could you call me 'Buck'?"

Mickey continued to refer to the Yankees manager as "Bucky" over the next several minutes of conversation.

Showalter finally repeated his request not to call him "Bucky," as in Bucky Dent, but just "Buck."

*Mickey and Mickey Jr. show off their batting styles near their Dallas home. Mickey Jr. also played professional baseball for a while.* Photo courtesy of Ozzie Sweet.

Mickey paused for several seconds, and with a wry look on his face, said, "Sure, Bucky."

Showalter turned around and smashed his fist on the top of the table in the booth, sending dishes and glasses flying. *"God damn it, Mickey,"* he exploded. *"Don't call me Bucky!"*

## EDDIE LAYTON

**Eddie Layton has been the Yankees organist since 1967. He has performed in soap operas for years, taught the organ, represented the Hammond Organ Company, performed at Radio City Music Hall, and entertained millions with his musical talents.**

---

"Mike Burke was the Yankee owner then, and he wanted to jazz up things at the Stadium because the team was bad. He hired me in 1967 and agreed to send a car for me to bring me to the Stadium and home every day. I thought it was a good deal. I didn't know anything about baseball. I played a couple of tunes when the players batted, and then Mickey got up. He hit the first pitch for a home run. I saw him run toward first base. I thought they were supposed to run toward third. I started yelling. Boy, was I embarrassed. A few days later I introduced myself to Mickey on the bench. I told him I didn't know anything about baseball and informed him that I yelled when I thought he ran off in the wrong direction. He never stopped laughing."

## JOE PEPITONE

**Joe Pepitone played for the Yankees as a first baseman and outfielder from 1962 through 1969. Pepitone works for the Yankees in their community relations department.**

"We were playing in Texas and Mickey invited me to the movies on an off day. We went to see *The Last Picture Show*, which was a very sad movie about how tough life was in this small, quiet Texas town. I didn't know anything about that. I was from Brooklyn. We came out of the theater and Mickey was in tears. I mean he was really bawling with a handkerchief in front of his face. I had never seen anything like that. I asked him, 'What's wrong, Mick?' He said, 'That movie could have been about my hometown of Commerce, Oklahoma. We had old movie houses just like that. I couldn't stand those old memories.'

"Then *I* started crying."

## MARY LAVAGETTO

**Mary Lavagetto was the wife of former big-league third baseman, coach, and Washington manager Cookie Lavagetto. She was friendly with Edna and Casey Stengel. They had their California and baseball backgrounds in common. She attended the famous hearing of the United States Senate Subcommittee on Antitrust Legislation and Monopoly in Washington on July 8, 1958. It was chaired by Senator Estes Kefauver of Tennessee, the vice presidential candidate in 1956 on the Democratic ticket led by Adlai Stevenson.**

"The room was jammed," Mary Lavagetto remembered in an interview recalling the hearings several years later, "and Casey seemed very jumpy. I sat with Edna and tried to calm her down."

"Mr. Stengel," began Kefauver, "you are the manager of the New York Yankees. Will you give us very briefly your background and your views on this legislation?"

"Well, I started in professional baseball in 1910," began the 68-year-old skipper of the Yankees. "I have been in professional ball, I would say, for 48 years." Casey motored on throughout his long and illustrious career in the game. Finally, after more than an hour of discussion of his life and career, another senator interrupted to ask Stengel directly whether or not he thought baseball needed the legislation the committee was considering.

"No," replied Stengel. The audience howled uproariously at the brevity of Stengel's final remark.

"Thank you very much," intoned Kefauver in his senatorial way.

Then Mickey Mantle, wearing a new suit, a striped tie, and a sheepish grin, was ushered to the table behind a set of microphones. "I could see he was certainly not going to get serious after *Casey's* performance," said Mary Lavagetto.

"Mr. Mantle," Kefauver asked the kid from Oklahoma, "do you have any observations with reference to the applicability of antitrust laws to baseball?"

"My views," said Mantle with that famous grin, "are just about the same as Casey's."

"The entire audience screamed," said Mary Lavagetto. "It was just about the funniest thing I had ever seen."

Mary Lavagetto loved to tell her husband—and anybody else who would listen—about the Senate session. Mickey Mantle's one-line speech at the hearing became as famous to some as Abraham Lincoln's two-minute oration in Gettysburg in 1863.

## GEORGE WEISS

**George Weiss was the longtime farm director and general manager of the Yankees. He hired Casey Stengel as the Yankees manager in 1949 after working with Stengel in the minor leagues. He was known as Lonesome George, a**

**tight-mouthed executive, and was famous for trying to sign all his players as cheaply as possible. He was paid extra by the Yankees if he kept the salary level below a specified amount each year.**

---

"All you have to do in a tough negotiation," Weiss once said in the days before the players organized into a strong union under chief executive Marvin Miller, "is wait them out. When they live up north and it's snow and ice in their hometown and the team is gathering in Florida, that's your best negotiating weapon."

Mickey Mantle won the Triple Crown in 1956 with a .353 average, 52 homers, and 130 runs batted in. The next season he batted .365. Ted Williams won the 1957 batting title with a .388 mark. "When I went in to negotiate after the 1957 season," Mantle reminisced at a New York Baseball Writers dinner during the early nineties, "I thought I would get a huge raise. We had won again and I had improved my Triple Crown batting average. You know what? George wanted to cut me. He said I didn't win the Triple Crown in 1957 and my home runs and RBIs were down. I couldn't believe it."

After the dinner, Mickey went back to Mickey Mantle's restaurant. He was still steaming about that horrible salary experience of almost 40 years earlier and the cheapness of George Weiss. "You know," Mickey bellowed to a crowd around his favorite table, "if the bastard wasn't dead, I'd kill him."

## MARTY APPEL

**Marty Appel served the Yankees for 20 years—first as public relations director, later as television producer for WPIX. He began in 1968 answering Mickey's fan mail. He is the author of 16 books, including his memoir, *Now Pitching for the Yankees*, and operates Marty Appel Public Relations.**

*Mickey and Ted Williams compare notes during the 1956 season, Mick's Triple Crown year.*
Photo courtesy of AP/Wide World Photos.

"My relationship with Mickey Mantle began with my first
Yankee job—answering his fan mail while on summer break
from college. He got hundreds of letters a day, almost all the
same—'You're my favorite player. Can I have your autograph?'
I'd search the stack for mail that I needed to pull aside to go
over with him 'personally' so that I could have some quality
time with him. He knew that was a big joke, that I was just
pretending the bar mitzvah invitations were important, so it
became a running gag that when he'd see me come into the
clubhouse he'd say, 'Do I have to get my bar mitzvah suit
pressed?' If he was in a good mood and not bothered by
injuries he could be very funny about the letters. When he
was hurting or in a slump, he could be pretty grouchy. Most
of those letters wound up in the garbage. Every so often there
would be a letter about a sick kid and Mickey would really be
touched. You could see the emotion in his face. With all his
problems, he related to that. It was just a thrill for me to sit
with Mickey.

"He took a liking to me, and as my pal Joe Garagiola Jr.
once said, 'No matter what we might accomplish in baseball,
it all comes down to, Mickey Mantle knows our names.' He
was right, that was a remarkable thing in itself.

"When he was a spring-training coach, it was an annual
ritual that I picked him up at the airport and we went to get
lunch and pick up his rental car together. That was pretty
much the best part of my day. We'd have terrific, personal
conversations in the car. 'Got a girlfriend?' he'd want to know.
I'd tell him the latest. Once I mentioned Merlyn, and he
sighed, 'Hell, she's my best friend! You need a girlfriend who's
gonna be your best friend.'"

"He came back to coach in September of 1970. He just
missed the game so much, he left NBC for this silly assign-
ment in which he coached first base in innings four, five, six,
spelling Ellie Howard. It embarrassed Ellie, and Mickey wasn't

too happy about that. He was raised in dust bowl Oklahoma, and you might think he was raised with segregated thoughts, but he loved Ellie and was always great with him. And he didn't want to embarrass him this way. That month of coaching was his last association with the 'regular-season' team.

"In spring training, he would find himself a little out of place as well. He wasn't the sort who could walk up to a player and say, 'Let me show you something.' And of course, the players were too in awe to approach him, save for a few. A typical spring-training ritual was rookie players coming to me and asking me to arrange for a photo of them with Mick. He was always gracious, and he'd always say something outrageous to get a big smile on their faces. Very outrageous.

"Merlyn had a little stroke once. It was in the papers. When I saw him, some months later, I asked how she was doing. 'She's fine,' he said. 'She just can't do this anymore,' and he pantomimed an intimate act for me.

"When Yankee Stadium opened in 1976, he was part of the row of celebrities lined up along the base line for the festivities. Just as we were approaching the ceremonial first pitch and I was lining up guys on the mound, he appeared right next to me, having strolled over from his spot. 'You all know a girl name of Angell?' he asked.

"It was someone I did know, and he had met her in Lake Tahoe. Suddenly, in front of sixty thousand people, he thought he had to mention this to me. It was at once my greatest moment—Mickey and I knew the same girl!—and my most embarrassing. 'Mick, get back to your spot! We've got a stadium to open here!' was all I could muster.

"During his one-month coaching stint in 1970, he wandered in one day and said, 'Marty, the Mick is sick.' He asked if I could go to the pressroom and get him a little pick-me-up beverage in a paper cup to help him recover. I loved that 'the Mick is sick' line.

"He was always uncomfortable around Joe DiMaggio, never knew what to say. It was as though it was always going to be 1951—the legend and the rookie, with Joe having nothing to say to Mickey. They'd shake hands, exchange 'how ya doin's,' but then there was never another sentence they could think of. Nothing about common experiences in travel, in golf tournaments, people they knew, etc. It was a generation and cultural gap, and they were both uncomfortable with it. At last Mickey found enormous amusement out of the flap over who would be introduced last on Old Timers' Day. He could care less. He was never interested in the politics of life. The fact that Joe was offended that Mickey would be introduced last, which happened once and only once, was something Mickey could always have fun with. Make sure you say 'greatest living muff diver,' he'd say, in response to Joe's insistence on 'greatest living player.'

"I got him to play center field one year at Old Timers' Day, the last time he was out there, and actually, the first time he was out there since he left the position after the 1966 season. He looked at me like I was nuts. 'You want me to go all the way out there?'

"'Yeah,' I said, 'that's where you belong! It'll be fantastic. Besides, you're being punished for losing your uniform.' It was true; we had sent him a No. 7 for an appearance somewhere, and he lost it. He was supposed to bring it with him to New York for this event. So I had Pete Sheehy put him in a Gene Michael jersey—17—and put a piece of athletic tape over the 1. He was 7, but it was not in the center of his back, and it looked very strange. But it worked. And he played one inning in center field that day, as a punishment, and it was great."

---

"Mickey was traveling on business to California. He got to Hollywood and went to dinner in one of those fashionable show business restaurants. His female assistant had picked it out. She was starstruck. While they were having dinner she began telling Mickey that the only show business personality she really cared about was Tom Selleck, the guy who starred on *Magnum P. I.* and a few movies. She kept talking about Selleck and suddenly looked over to the side of the room. Believe it or not, there was Tom Selleck. He looked over and spotted Mickey. Like any awestruck baseball fan, he got up from his seat and slowly came over to where Mickey was sitting. 'Mickey,' he began, 'I'm Tom Selleck and I know this is very impolite of me and I've been through this kind of stuff, but I just wanted to meet you. You have been my hero ever since I was a kid. It's such a thrill to meet you.' Mickey just stared at him. He probably didn't have the slightest idea who Selleck was, and he was totally unimpressed. The only television Mickey watched was sports and soap operas. He had his answer ready. 'Hey, Selleck, you wanna meet my assistant?'"

## MEL ALLEN

**Mel Allen (no relation to the coauthor) was the Yankees broadcaster from 1939 through 1964. He was fired after the 1964 season by new GM Ralph Houk. The real reason was never revealed.**

---

"I was brought back to the Stadium for the first time by new Yankee owner Michael Burke on Mickey Mantle Day in 1969," Allen said in a 1980 interview. "I was just thrilled. Everybody who had anything to do with Mickey's career was there. That included Tom Greenwade, who had signed him in Oklahoma, and two of his minor league managers, Harry Craft and George Selkirk. There were so many of his old teammates and friends and family on the field. I introduced Mickey by calling him, 'That magnificent Yankee, No. 7, Mickey Mantle.' What a roar went up from the full house in the Stadium. It just seemed to go on and on and Mickey just stood there with his head down staring at the ground. He looked up every so often and watched as the crowd stood and applauded. Finally he got

*The legend and the rookie: Mickey and Joe DiMaggio in 1951.*
Photo courtesy of AP/Wide World Photos.

to the microphone and thanked the fans and his teammates and said how he now understood what Lou Gehrig felt on his farewell day and how he understood now Lou's phrase about being the luckiest man on the face of the Earth. It was just so emotional, so touching, so big a day in the Yankee tradition."

"That had to be one of the highlights of my life," Mickey said in an interview years later. "I never stopped crying. It was as if I was a stranger up there, as if the years I played were part of somebody else's career."

"I never forgot that day," broadcaster Allen said. "I had a wonderful career, but that had to be one of the standouts. *Mickey Mantle Day.* It still gives me chills to say it."

## RALPH HOUK

**Ralph Houk played for the Yankees as a backup catcher from 1947 through 1954 after a heroic World War II career as a U.S. Ranger major—later his baseball nickname. The Major managed the Yankees from 1961 through 1964, served as general manager, and then managed the Yankees one last time from 1966 through 1973. He later managed Detroit.**

---

"I liked to kid around with the players a lot, especially before games. I thought it helped relax them. One time I was showing a few of the guys how a catcher in the minors went after a foul ball and spun around a few times looking for it before the ball landed about 10 feet away from him. He was so embarrassed he started digging a little hole in the ground with his hands, and he grabbed the baseball and stuck it into the dirt. Everybody was laughing like crazy. Mickey was laughing the loudest. 'Holy gee, skip, holy gee.' He had the kind of laugh that just put everybody in a good mood."

# JULIUS ISAACSON

**Julius Y. Isaacson was the president of the Allied Novelty Workers Union and of the AFL-CIO for more than 25 years. During his stewardship, the union boasted more than fifty-five thousand members. He was a great friend of many Yankees players including Roger Maris and Mickey Mantle, and he served as a consultant on the HBO film _61*_. Liederman first met "Big Julie," a giant of a man who could still play defensive end for the Giants, in 1988, a few months prior to the opening of his restaurant. Some rogue union plumbers tried to strong-arm their way into the job, offering services that were close to completion by other plumbers. When Liederman mentioned this to Mickey (who hated all unions due to his dad's mining experiences in Oklahoma), he said, "Call Big Julie; he'll lose those guys." Liederman did, and Julie delivered: the work was completed by nonunion plumbers. His granddaughter, Stacey Callahan, is now a manager at Mickey Mantle's.**

---

"I rented the apartment for Mickey, Roger, and Bob Cerv at 86-25 Van Wyck Expressway in Queens, New York. Mickey loved country-and-western music, and any time I went over there, Mickey would be listening to Johnny Cash, George Jones, Patsy Cline, or the like. It was all Greek to me. He kept his records in a stack by the turntable, and one day I topped his collection with a few of my favorite Jewish music records, featuring chart-toppers such as 'Hava Nagila' and 'Dreidel, Dreidel, Dreidel.' Customarily Mickey always went straight for the Victrola after returning home from the ballpark (win or lose), picked the top record from the pile, and dropped it onto the turntable before crashing on his easy chair. This time, 'Hava Nagila' blared from the speakers, much to Mickey's bewilderment. After a few notes, a playfully disgruntled Mick bounded over to the machine, took the record off, stepped outside, and tossed it across the Van Wyck. I was laughing too hard to be pissed off, but every time I saw Mickey after that day, he would bust out singing the chorus to 'Hava Nagila.'

"During the filming of Mickey and Roger's movie *Safe at Home*, they invited me to come down to Florida with my wife, and we ended up with walk-on parts in the film. Initially, Mickey and Roger struggled through their scenes, necessitating take after take. However, once they got the hang of it, they were naturals. As they waited for their next action cue, Mickey and Roger watched a scene wherein a diminutive umpire stood behind the plate as a sliding player tried to score. His only f***ing line was, 'Safe at home!' which, of course, was the title of the movie. Time after time, the tiny actor blew the take by fumbling his line. 'S-s-safe at home,' he stammered. 'Hafe in shome! S-s-safe in the home!' I don't know what his problem was, but for some reason, the poor guy just didn't get it. Every time he blew his line, the player sliding into home had to get up, dust himself off, and return to third base to do it all over again. Mickey was getting restless after a while, and finally, he called out to Oscar Frawley, the actor who was playing the club's manager. 'Hey, Oscar,' he roared. 'Who's that f***in' dummy in the ump's uniform?'

" 'Mickey,' Oscar replied, 'that's the guy that put up all the money to make this picture!' "

---

"Even though I had the deeper pockets in those days, Mickey always picked up the tab anywhere we went. Despite his rough-hewn reputation, he was by far the most generous guy on the team.

"The day Roger hit his 61st in '61, he insisted on visiting Mickey right after the game in his hospital room, before he went off into the night to celebrate. Mick had dropped out of the home-run race with 54 due to an infected hip, and he spent the rest of the regular season in the hospital. When Roger and I arrived, Mickey limped out of bed and gave Roger a huge hug.

"One day in the clubhouse after the game, Mick was presented with two dozen baseballs to be signed for the team's owner, Dan Topping. I was there with a request for a photo with the blind, nine-year-old son of one of my union members, wondering if Mick would understand why a blind kid would want a photo he'd never be able to look at. Mickey understood perfectly. He reached down, picked up the baseballs from the Yankee brass, and threw them across the locker room into the Dumpster. 'F*** Topping,' he snapped, only half kidding. Then, turning his full attention to the child, he posed for several photos and gave him a game-used, autographed ball and bat as well.

"Mickey's favorite practical joke was putting live firecrackers into his teammates' shoes—and speaking of dancing feet, I went with Mickey, Roger, and Billy Martin once when they appeared on the *Arthur Murray Dance Show* to dance with a couple of lucky members of the live studio audience. Billy was too drunk to dance, and Mickey cursed him out. Mickey didn't really know how to dance, but he faked it. Too bad they didn't play 'Hava Nagila.'

"In spring training back in those days, the Yankees stayed at the Yankee Clipper Hotel in Fort Lauderdale. One year, Arnold Palmer and Jack Nicklaus were in town for a golf tournament and I arranged for Mickey and Roger to meet the two budding legends at a nearby driving range. I sat there amazed as Mick repeatedly outdrove the two astonished and admiring professional golfers."

*Mickey is joined by Senator Robert F. Kennedy before a game at Yankee Stadium. They were two of the most beloved figures in American history.* Photo courtesy of the New York Yankees.

# Mantle as Legend

## BILLY CRYSTAL

**Billy Crystal, actor, comedian, Academy Award ceremony host, stand-up comic, and inveterate Yankees fan, grew up in Long Beach, Long Island, New York. By the time he was 10 years old, in 1957, he was hooked on the Yankees in general and Mickey Mantle in particular. Crystal is seen often in his movies and in his Hollywood office wearing a Yankees cap with the poster of his film on the great home-run year, *61\**, on a nearby wall.**

Crystal attended the memorabilia auction at Sotheby's in 1999 of Yankees part-owner Barry Halper's collection. He sat quietly in the front row of the auction house until a 1960 glove used by Mickey was put up for bidding. After spirited bidding, Crystal bought the glove for $118,000. He immediately went upstairs to the suite where Halper was sitting to phone his mother about the purchase.

"Mom, I just bought a Mickey Mantle glove," Crystal told his elderly mother.

"How much did you pay?"

"I paid $118,000," Crystal said.

There was a long pause on the other end of the phone.

Then Crystal's mother asked, "What was wrong with the glove we bought you at Davega's for five dollars?"

## BILL KANE

**Bill Kane worked for the Yankees from 1961 through 1996 as a statistician, radio producer, traveling secretary, and assistant to George Steinbrenner. He was hit with polio as a youngster but became a serious sports fan during his recovery. He graduated from St. Bonaventure with a degree in statistics and was hired by the Yankees despite his severe limp. He became known as Killer Kane, a kidding nickname for a sweet guy, when another Bill, manager Bill Virdon, took over the team in 1974.**

---

"I was having a few pops in a bar in Detroit one night and a guy came over to me and asked me for my autograph. He said I had to be Mickey Mantle because I had blond hair, looked just like the Mick, and was sitting in a bar. I told him I wasn't Mickey. He was a little drunk and he just insisted I was the Mick and demanded I sign this autograph for him.

"He was such a pain in the ass I figured I could only get rid of him by signing. I scribbled Mickey's name and just turned away. Then I got up to go to the bathroom. The guy saw me limping away and barely able to move on my own. 'Gee, Mick, I knew your leg was bad but not like this. Wow, how could you be this great with a leg like that?' The next day I told Mickey the story. He couldn't stop laughing."

## BURT REYNOLDS

One of the most popular and loved movie, television, and theater stars of the 20ᵗʰ century, Burt Reynolds was a Florida high school football star and later a fine player at Florida State University. He went to school with Dick Howser, who later became a manager with the New York Yankees and Kansas City A's. Reynolds often visited spring training when Howser was the manager. In the new Burt Reynolds Museum in his hometown of Jupiter, Florida, there is a wonderful photo of Reynolds and Mickey.

———————

"It was a thrill to meet Mickey Mantle. He had stopped playing by the time I got to know him, but he still looked like a classic athlete, handsome, broad shoulders, strong arms and legs. If you could create the perfect picture of an athlete it was Mickey Mantle. I wish they had made a movie of Mickey's life. I would have loved to play him when I was a little younger. Hell, I would have loved to have been him."

## DONALD TRUMP

The famed New York builder, entrepreneur, and bon vivant, Donald Trump grew up in Brooklyn but became a Yankees fan in the early seventies when George Steinbrenner bought the Yankees and invited Trump to watch a game from his private Stadium box.

———————

"I got to meet Mickey on one of those Yankee Old Timers' Games. I had seen him play when I was a kid, but this was just exciting for me to be sitting next to him and talking to him. You could see he was really something special by the way everybody gathered around him. George likes stars. There never was a bigger star than Mickey."

# GEORGE PLIMPTON

**Famed writer and editor George Plimpton went to his first baseball game at the Polo Grounds in 1937 to see the New York Giants. Left-handed pitcher Cliff Melton pitched a great game. He had a looping left-handed style and big ears. "I decided that day I wanted to be a left-handed pitcher with big ears," Plimpton said. Plimpton died in 2003.**

---

"I remember a time when the poet Marianne Moore came to a Yankee game with me at the invitation of Yankee owner Mike Burke. The Yankees were playing the Red Sox. Bill Monbouquette was pitching for Boston. Miss Moore noticed he kept pulling at his genitalia. She said, 'That's perfect. *Monbouquette* means my "little bundle."' She didn't know a lot about baseball, but we had fun. My favorite day at the Stadium was the great heavyweight fight in 1955 when Rocky Marciano knocked out Archie Moore. I later got in the ring with Archie Moore and wrote an article about it for *Sports Illustrated*. In the next year, 1956, Mickey Mantle had his best season with the Triple Crown. I don't think any baseball player ever had a better season. It was just so much fun to watch Mickey play. I don't think there was ever a player with a greater connection to the fans than Mickey Mantle."

# HENRY KISSINGER

**The former secretary of state and presidential adviser was born in Furth, Germany, and came to the United States in 1938. Henry Kissinger was 15 when he settled into the Washington Heights section of Manhattan. He soon had a part-time job after school in a Bronx shaving brush factory. Kissinger won the Nobel Peace Prize for helping end the Vietnam War and remains active as a consultant to**

**many companies and governments. He often attends games at Yankee Stadium as George Steinbrenner's guest.**

---

"Most of the workers in the factory were Italians and were always talking about baseball and about their favorite player, Joe DiMaggio. One day they took me to a game at Yankee Stadium, and I became a big fan. I followed the game when I went to Harvard, while I was in the army, and even when I was overseas on assignments for the government.

"I started out as a Yankee fan rooting for DiMaggio, especially because my Italian friends were always talking about him. Then I began going to games with my own friends. Mickey Mantle soon became my favorite. I liked Yogi Berra and Whitey Ford, but there was always something so commanding about Mickey Mantle. Baseball has meant a lot to me. Imagine, a kid like me from Germany getting to see Joe DiMaggio and Mickey Mantle and even later getting to know them. I could never even dream of something like that. And I couldn't dream of being the secretary of state of the United States, either."

## PAT COOPER

**One of the most entertaining comics over the past four decades, Pat Cooper has been a baseball fan all his life and has always loved Mickey Mantle.**

---

"Mickey Mantle? I thought his name was Mickey Mantello. Ain't he Italian? I always thought he was. He's got those muscles. You don't start up with a guy like that. My friends Yogi and Rizzuto, they always told me he was a *goombar*. I just want to go on record as saying he was my favorite. That's after DiMaggio. I remember when I was a kid and they

95

had a picture of Joe cooking spaghetti. What did Mickey cook? Oklahoma corn dogs. Anyway, we loved Mickey and we miss him around here."

## TOMMY LASORDA

**A Hall of Famer, Tommy Lasorda was one of the great managers in the history of the game. He started his career as a pitcher in the Brooklyn Dodgers organization, but lost his roster spot on the Dodgers in 1955 to a kid left-hander the Dodgers had to protect named Sandy Koufax. He faced Mickey often in spring-training games when the Brooklyn Dodgers would play the New York Yankees.**

---

"Mickey was one of those legends in the game. You just wanted to go up and ask him for his autograph whenever you ran into him. He loved to laugh and we spent a lot of time telling stories with each other when we would meet at baseball banquets. I remember when he was fronting for that casino down in Atlantic City and I was invited there for a banquet one winter. He was always so much fun to be around. You know what? I wish the Dodgers had him."

## WILLIE MAYS

**Many observers of the game consider Willie Mays the best player the sport has ever seen. He started out with the Giants in 1951 and was a scared rookie when Bobby Thomson hit his famous homer off Ralph Branca. He was the guy who hit the fly ball to right-center that Joe DiMaggio called Mickey off in the 1951 Series. It caused Mickey to tear up his knee.**

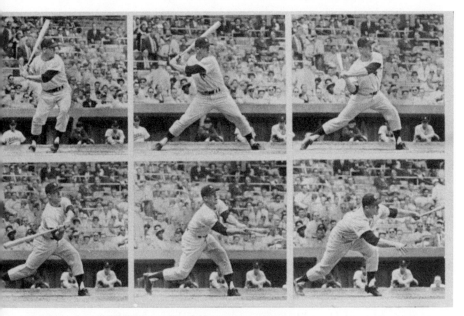

*Mickey pokes a hit off Kansas City Athletics starter Tommy Lasorda at Yankee Stadium on June 6, 1956.* Photo courtesy of AP/Wide World Photos.

"See, we had this rivalry, when I first came up, me, Mickey, and Duke Snider over in Brooklyn. We were about the same age, and me and Mickey came up the same year, 1951, and all the sportswriters were comparing us: Willie, Mickey, and the Duke. The New York writers started that and it really caught on. They even have a Willie, Mickey, and the Duke award at their baseball dinner every winter.

"I remember the last time I saw Mickey, in 1995 at that dinner when they made the award and named it for us. I was in tears when I talked about it because I knew now my name would last forever in New York with that award. Mickey got up after me and he didn't say much. He just told the crowd that he agreed with me and he was pretty emotional about having an award named after us."

## REGIS PHILBIN

**A television personality for almost 50 years, singer, comedian, and talk show host Regis Philbin has been a fan of the Yankees ever since his childhood—he grew up near the stadium in the Bronx.**

"I was a Joe DiMaggio guy when I was a little kid. Wasn't everybody? Then Mickey came along with that handsome face, that blond hair, and those massive home runs from both sides of the plate. Don't you think every kid in my neighborhood dreamed of growing up to be Mickey Mantle? I didn't become Mickey Mantle, but I got to meet him. That was enough for me."

## TOM SEAVER

**Known as "Tom Terrific" and "the Franchise" in his pitching days with the Mets, Tom Seaver won 311 games with a 2.86 ERA and 3,640 strikeouts in 20 big-league seasons. He won three Cy Young Awards and was elected to baseball's Hall of Fame in 1992.**

---

"I wanted to drive across the country from my home in Fresno [California] in 1960 when I was 15 years old with some friends. I wanted to see Mickey Mantle and I wanted to see Yankee Stadium. My parents wouldn't let me do it. I had to wait until I was pitching for the Mets in 1967 before I could get to see Mantle. I faced him in a couple of spring-training games in 1967 and 1968, and I can't remember what I did against him. I was just too overwhelmed by pitching against him after I had always dreamed of playing on the same field with him. I never did."

## MARVIN MILLER

**Marvin Miller was the executive director of the Major League Baseball Players Association for 16 years and led the players to the promised land, free agency.**

---

"I remember the first time I walked into a Yankee spring-training camp. I addressed the players and I was putting my notes together and looked up to see only two people in the clubhouse, Joe DiMaggio and Mickey Mantle. DiMaggio was wearing an old, battered Yankee uniform as a special instructor, and Mickey sat in the corner of the clubhouse unwrapping his bandages on his sore legs. This was DiMaggio and Mantle and nobody was around to help them and the conditions were terrible. I knew then how much the players needed an association and how much we could help improve conditions around the ballpark."

## GEORGE STEINBRENNER

**The Yankees owner purchased the team in a limited partnership in 1973. He brought the Yankees their first pennant in 12 years in 1976 and their first World Series title in 15 years in 1977. The Yankees won four more titles under Steinbrenner's manager Joe Torre in 1996, 1998, 1999, and 2000.**

---

"I was a big Joe DiMaggio fan as a kid growing up in Cleveland. I always came to town for a game and hung around the hotel for DiMaggio's autograph. I was already in business when Mickey started playing for the Yankees in 1951. I followed his career and wished we could have him in Cleveland. I always enjoyed seeing him at spring training and on Old Timers' Days. One of the most thrilling days ever was in 1978 when Mickey and Roger Maris came back to the Stadium to raise the World Series flag."

## MATT GALANTE

**Matt Galante, born in Brooklyn, was signed by the New York Yankees organization in 1966 after an All-America college career at St. John's University in New York. He never made it to the big leagues, but he has been a long-time coach in the Houston organization and with the New York Mets.**

---

"When I started with the Yankees we all knew we wanted to grow up to be Mickey Mantle. Even a little guy like me who didn't hit home runs [nine in one season at a small ballpark in Binghamton in 1968 was his professional career output] because Mickey was the best. I still get a kick when we play the Yankees just looking out at center field, looking at those monuments out there and knowing that was Mickey's home for so many years."

## MO VAUGHN

**Mo Vaughn is from Norwalk, Connecticut. He starred in college baseball at Seton Hall University in New Jersey and was signed by the Boston Red Sox in 1989. He hit as many as 44 home runs for the Red Sox in 1996. He played three years for Anaheim and joined the New York Mets as their first baseman in 2001.**

---

"I hit a lot of balls into the third deck at Yankee Stadium, just like Mickey did. Most of them were in batting practice, but a few were in there in games. Guys used to kid me and call me the 'new Mickey.' That was fun to hear. The only difference was Mickey did it from the right side as well as the left side. That tells you how great he was."

## JOE TORRE

**Joe Torre, a Brooklyn native, broke into baseball as a chubby catcher with the Milwaukee Braves in 1960. He hit .297 in an 18-year career as a catcher, first baseman, and third baseman with the Braves, the Cardinals, and the Mets. He managed the Mets, Braves, and Cardinals before being appointed manager of the Yankees in 1996. He won**

**four World Series titles in his first seven seasons as field
leader of the Yankees.**

---

"When I was a kid we were scheduled to play a sandlot
championship game at the Stadium while the Yankees were on
the road. That was just so thrilling. Then it rained and the
game was pushed back a week. We had to play across the
street from the Stadium at Macombs Dam Park. The Yankees
were playing that day. We suddenly heard a huge roar from
across the street. Everybody knew what it was. Mickey had hit
a homer. You could always tell by the noise of the crowd. One
of the kids had a portable radio, and a few seconds later, he
begins yelling, 'Mickey hit a homer.' We all look at him with
scorn and one guy says, 'We know. We know. We heard the
crowd.' It was always easy to hear Mickey's homers."

## LEE MAZZILLI

**Lee Mazzilli hit .259 in 14 big-league seasons with the
Mets, Texas, the Yankees, Pittsburgh, and Toronto. He was
a valuable role player on the 1986 world champion Mets.
He was a handsome kid from Brooklyn with a distinct
swagger as a player and was often called "the Italian
Stallion." He became a Yankees coach since 2000 and is
now the manager of the Baltimore Orioles.**

---

"I grew up in Brooklyn in the sixties as a switch-hitter.
Mickey Mantle was my hero. Who else could it be? I even
wore my pants the way Mickey did. I got so nervous the first
time I walked on the field at Yankee Stadium. I just looked
out there and could see Mickey Mantle. He's gone a long time
now and I still see him in center field. I am weird, right?"

*Willie, Mickey, and the Duke: (from left) Duke Snider, Willie Mays, and Mick, all Hall of Fame center fielders. Mickey and Willie joined their teams (and Snider in New York) in 1951.*
Photo courtesy of Jackson Pokress.

## JOE FRANKLIN

**Joe Franklin, the King of Nostalgia, has been a longtime radio and television personality with a specialty in former stars.**

---

"I got the guy who owned Mickey's first home-run ball to auction off the ball in my restaurant. Mickey hit it in Chicago, May 6, 1951. I always loved Mickey. Who didn't? I wish I owned the ball. At least it was done here in my Eighth Avenue place. What a thrill! Just being connected with anything Mickey did was a thrill."

## ROBERT MERRILL

**Robert Merrill is one of the great opera performers of the 20th century. He is a native of Brooklyn, New York, and grew up as a Dodgers fan. He became friendly with Yankees owner George Steinbrenner when Steinbrenner bought the Yankees in 1973. Steinbrenner asked Merrill to sing the national anthem at Yankee Stadium that year, and he has been doing it ever since in person or by recording.**

---

"I rooted against Mickey as a Dodger fan because he used to beat us all the time. Then I met him once in George's box at the Stadium on Opening Day. He was so beautiful to look at, so powerful a man and so much fun to talk to. He became my favorite Yankee.

"I sang the national anthem one time at the Stadium before a sellout crowd. One of the newspapermen wrote, 'Robert Merrill is the Mickey Mantle of singers.' I think that was a greater thrill than singing at La Scala."

# Len Berman

**Len Berman has been a sportscaster in New York for many years. The first time he went to the stadium as a kid, he sat under the press box. A foul ball came into the press box and sportswriter Stan Isaacs of *Newsday* dropped it to him. That was his greatest Yankee Stadium thrill.**

---

"I never covered Mickey when he was playing, but I interviewed him many times on Old Timers' Days and Opening Days. He was always funny. He cursed a lot before you started rolling, and that always worried you. But once you were live he was a perfect gentleman and very funny. I think I would get more feedback from a Mickey Mantle interview than from anybody else except maybe Muhammad Ali."

# Teresa Wright

**Teresa Wright starred as Lou Gehrig's wife, Eleanor, in *The Pride of the Yankees*, the 1942 drama about the great Yankees first baseman. She also won an Academy Award as a supporting actress for her role in *Mrs. Miniver*. She lives in Norwalk, Connecticut, and attended her first ever New York Baseball Writers dinner in 1999—the session that marked the 60th anniversary of Gehrig's retirement from the Yankees.**

---

"George Steinbrenner invited me to attend the opening game at Yankee Stadium that year [1999] and throw out the first ball. I told him I would do it if he allowed me to bring my grandson along—he's a real baseball fan. We sat in Mr. Steinbrenner's box and talked about the Yankees. I told Mr. Steinbrenner I really didn't even know who Lou Gehrig was when we made the movie. He was surprised. I knew who Joe DiMaggio was because he married Marilyn Monroe and she was a Hollywood star. I also told him I knew who Mickey Mantle was. He was just an exciting, handsome personality. I was surprised they didn't make a film of Mickey Mantle's life. I would have loved to play his wife, also."

## BOWIE KUHN

**Bowie Kuhn was the commissioner of baseball from 1969 through 1984. He was an attorney with the New York law firm of Willkie Farr & Gallagher for many years. He grew up in Washington, D.C.**

---

"I was a scoreboard boy for the old Washington Senators. I always loved the game. I remember the game when Mickey hit the longest home run ever off Chuck Stobbs in old Griffith Stadium. In 1961 I was working in New York. I went to many games that year as I watched the Maris/Mantle home-run chase. Mickey was always one of my favorite players. It was very sad when I had to suspend him in 1983 for connecting with a gambling casino. I guess he needed the money. I had to do it. To me, the game's integrity is everything."

## DON SUTTON

**Don Sutton won 324 games in 23 seasons. He was elected to baseball's Hall of Fame in 1998 and has spent many years as a broadcaster. He grew up in rural Alabama near the Florida border.**

---

"I always played at being Mickey with the No. 7 when I was a kid. I always wanted to sign with the Yankees and play with Mickey. I played first base and I pitched. A Yankee scout named Atley Donald came by to look at me. He said I didn't throw hard enough to be signed. That broke my heart.

"I walked into Yankee Stadium for the first time as a big leaguer and I could see the ghosts of Babe Ruth and Lou Gehrig and the rest. What was more important to me was the one fact that Mickey played there. I was standing in center field before my first game there. I could feel Mickey's presence."

## BUD SELIG

**Allan H. "Bud" Selig was a used-car salesman in his native Milwaukee when he purchased the failed one-season Seattle Pilots and brought them to Milwaukee as the Brewers. He ran the team until he took a leave of absence to become acting commissioner and then commissioner of baseball. He came to Yankee Stadium in the middle fifties.**

"My mother gave me a vacation trip to New York so we could go to Yankee Stadium. We sat way up in the left-field stands and peered down at the game. It was just so exciting because the Stadium was so enormous and seemed to stretch out for miles.

"I was 15 years old and Mickey Mantle was playing center field for the Yankees. It was 50 years ago but I can remember it like it was yesterday. Nobody ever forgets the first time they saw Mickey Mantle swing a bat or chase down a fly ball."

# ED LUCAS

**Ed Lucas was an 11-year-old kid growing up in Newark on October 3, 1951. The Dodgers were playing the Giants that day for the National League pennant. A ball struck him in the eye and blinded him for life. He is now a radio personality and freelance sportswriter despite his disability.**

---

"Phil Rizzuto worked in a clothing store in Newark. About six months after the accident I went there for some clothes and told him what a baseball fan I was. He invited me to visit him at the Stadium. He introduced me to all the players, including Mickey Mantle. I shook his hand and realized how strong he was. I remember sitting up in the press box in the sixties and listening to the games on the radio. I could always tell when Mickey hit a huge one out. The sounds in the stadium and through my headset would almost knock me out."

# SID ZION

**Sid Zion is a rambunctious newspaper columnist and freelance writer unafraid of taking on any political power structure. He started going to Yankee Stadium as a fan in the forties.**

---

"My favorite player was Tiny Bonham, the pitcher. I just loved his name. He was a huge guy but they called him Tiny. That was typical ballplayer humor. I stayed a Yankee fan, watched DiMaggio and all the rest, and then fell in love with Mantle. It was his name and the way he looked and the way he played. Mickey Mantle. It was like he was out of a fiction book."

## LEONARD KOPPETT

**Hall of Fame sportswriter Leonard Koppett grew up on 157th Street and Gerard Avenue in the Bronx, four blocks from Yankee Stadium. He resided in Palo Alto, California, until his death in 2003.**

———————

"I was taken to my first game in 1931, the Yankees versus the Boston Red Sox. Babe Ruth and Lou Gehrig were still playing. It was a sellout and we stood all nine innings. I can't even remember who won, but it was a thrill. We got home and I was playing outside with the other kids and suddenly we heard a roar from the Stadium. I couldn't figure out why. The game was over. One of the other kids told me they were playing a doubleheader. A doubleheader? Who knew? Then I became a sportswriter and was there on October 3, 1951, when Thomson hit the homer. I worked the desk that night and through the Series. I remember when Mickey got hurt. It was a big story because he was such a hot prospect. Mickey was always a big story."

## HILLARY RODHAM CLINTON

**Hillary Rodham Clinton, United States senator from New York and former First Lady, grew up in Park Ridge, Illinois, a Chicago suburb.**

———————

"I rooted for the Cubs, as did my family and most folks on our side of town," she wrote in her autobiography *Living History*. "My favorite was Mr. Cub himself, Ernie Banks. In our neighborhood, it was nearly sacrilegious to cheer for the rival White Sox of the American League, so I adopted the Yankees as my AL team, in part because I loved Mickey

Mantle. My explanations of Chicago sports rivalries fell on deaf ears during my senate campaign years later, when skeptical New Yorkers were incredulous that a Chicago native could claim youthful allegiance to a team from the Bronx."

## JOHNNY BENCH

**Hall of Fame catcher Johnny Bench anchored the Cincinnati Reds Big Red Machine for 17 seasons. Many observers consider Bench the best catcher the game has ever seen.**

---

"When I was a kid growing up in Oklahoma City I used to listen to the *Game of the Week* with the Yankees most every Saturday. One day I heard the announcer say that Mickey Mantle from Commerce, Oklahoma, was the best player in the game. I turned to my dad and said, 'Does that mean guys from Oklahoma can play in the big leagues?'

"When he said that was so, I decided then and there that is what I would do. Mickey Mantle changed my life."

## CHARLES E. SCHUMER

**The senior senator from New York, Charles E. Schumer, grew up in the Sheepshead Bay section of Brooklyn in the late fifties and early sixties. The Brooklyn Dodgers and the New York Giants had already moved west. Schumer became a fan of his beloved Yankees. Both Roger Maris and Mantle were idols of the senior senator from New York throughout their careers**

---

"I followed the 1961 pursuit of Babe Ruth's single-season home-run record," Schumer told sports columnist Ira Berkow of *The New York Times*. "I think Roger Maris deserves Hall of Fame recognition and should join Mickey in Cooperstown. He played with grit and determination but was also a class act."

## GARY CARTER

**Gary Carter was an outstanding catcher and leader with the Montreal Expos and world champion 1986 New York Mets as well as the Dodgers and Giants at the end of his career. He batted .262 over 19 seasons and was elected to baseball's Hall of Fame in 2003.**

---

On July 27, 2003, at his Cooperstown Hall of Fame induction, Carter said, "I grew up in Southern California. My idol was the Mick. Mickey, I know you are here today as I am being inducted to join you in the Baseball Hall of Fame."

## PEE WEE REESE

**Harold "Pee Wee" Reese was the Hall of Fame shortstop of the Brooklyn Dodgers, captain of the team, and a leader who helped Jackie Robinson make the transition into a big leaguer in 1947. Reese played 16 years with the Dodgers in Brooklyn and Los Angeles, went on to a coaching and broadcasting career alongside Dizzy Dean for many years, and was one of baseball's most popular figures. He died in 1999 at the age of 81.**

---

*Pee Wee Reese (right) and Mickey were combatants in seven World Series, with the Yankees winning all but one.* Photo courtesy of the New York Yankees.

Pee Wee Reese was visiting in Manhattan shortly before his death and came to Mickey Mantle's restaurant on Central Park South. Reese had played in seven World Series against the Yankees, winning only one time, in 1955.

"I want to see the owner," he told one of the servers at Mantle's.

"Soon Bill Liederman, who opened the restaurant with Mantle in 1988, walked up and greeted Pee Wee Reese warmly.

"I loved Mickey Mantle. I really loved him," Reese said, "but f*** the Yankees."

## JOHN MCENROE

**John McEnroe was probably the most exciting tennis player of all time with his gritty performances and outrageous conduct. He won every major tennis title except the French Open, was the dominant doubles player of his time with partner Peter Fleming (who once said, "The greatest doubles team is John McEnroe and anybody"), and serves as a broadcaster of most major tennis events. He still plays remarkably well on the senior tour. His best-selling autobiography with James Kaplan, titled *You Cannot Be Serious*, details his raw and wonderful life. McEnroe may also be New York's greatest sports fan as an attendee at so many games of the Yankees, Rangers, and Knicks.**

---

"My greatest sports hero of all time is Mickey Mantle. I just loved watching him. Every kid in my neighborhood in Douglaston [Queens, New York] wanted to grow up to be Mickey Mantle."

## HAROLD ROSENTHAL

**Harold Rosenthal covered the New York Yankees for the *New York Herald Tribune* for many years. He was one of the wittiest writers on the sports beat with many breaking stories, dozens of fine magazine articles, and several books. He died in 1998, at the age of 86, shortly after completing another magazine article—a working writer to the end.**

---

"Arthur 'Red' Patterson, the Yankee publicity director, had come up with the brainchild of writing rookies each winter at their homes and asking them to write back about themselves. These rookie stories would give the fans something to talk about, get the clubs a little publicity, and give the new player a little exposure," Rosenthal said during the early nineties.

"Patterson gave us the addresses of these kids. Some of them were only in Class B, and nobody expected them to make the Yankees in 1951. There was one kid who played at Joplin, a Class B team, and had a terrific year. Patterson said his name was Mantle, and the Yankees thought he had a pretty good chance to make the team as a shortstop. I had to laugh at that because the shortstop of the previous season, 1950, was Phil Rizzuto, who happened to be the MVP that year."

On January 8, 1951, Rosenthal received a letter addressed to him at the *New York Herald Tribune*. It was written in printed, block letters on the top of a lined white five-and-dime sheet of paper. The letter began with the greeting, "MISTER H. ROSENTHAL."

This was written by a boy of 19, who had graduated from high school a year and a half earlier, just after he turned 17. He had worked on the Commerce High newspaper because he knew so much about sports, but he had little interest in developing writing skills. Here was a youngster who, from his earliest years, was pointed in one direction only: to baseball.

*I WILL ANSWER YOUR LETTER
THAT I RECEIVED THE OTHER DAY.
YOU'LL HAVE TO PARDON THE PAPER
AND PENCIL.*

*TOM GREENWADE SIGNED ME
FROM THE BAXTER SPRINGS BAN
JOHNSON TEAM I WAS PLAYING ON.
MY BACKGROUND IN BASEBALL
WASN'T VERY MUCH BEFORE I GOT
INTO PRO BALL. I STARTED PLAYING
IN A GABBY STREET LEAGUE WHEN I
WAS 12 & PLAYED WITH BAXTER 2
YEARS AND THEN SIGNED WITH
INDEPENDENCE WHEN I GOT OUT OF
SCHOOL AT 17.*

*I DON'T HAVE ANY RELATIVES
PLAYING ANY SPORTS. I GUESS UNTIL
I WAS 17 I WAS A LOT BETTER FIELDER
THAN HITTER BECAUSE I WAS NEVER
MUCH BIGGER THAN A BASEBALL BAT.
BUT LAST SEASON I WOULD SAY MY
HITTING WAS BETTER THAN MY
FIELDING AS I LED THE LEAGUE IN
ERRORS WITH AN EVEN 50, BUT I ALSO
LED IN STRIKEOUTS SO IT'S ABOUT A
DRAW.*

*I HAVE ALWAYS PLAYED S.S. & PHIL
RIZZUTO WAS ALWAYS MY IDOL.*

*I GOT MY ANKLE KICKED IN FOOT-
BALL PRACTICE IN '46 & IT BRUISED
THE BONE & THAT CAUSED TB ON
THE BONE.*

*I'M NOT THE ONLY CHILD AS
THERE ARE 3 MORE BROTHERS AND A
SISTER IN OUR FAMILY. TWO OF MY
BROTHERS ARE TWINS & ARE GOING*

*TO BE GOOD ATHLETES. I'M THE OLD-
EST BUT THEY ARE ABOUT AS BIG.
WELL, I GUESS I'VE ANS. ALL THE
QUESTIONS FOR YOU, SO I'LL SAY
GOOD-BYE FOR NOW.*

The letter ended with a printed signature, "MICKEY MANTLE" in block letters.

The original of the letter now resides in the Oklahoma Sports Hall of Fame, where Rosenthal contributed it about 10 years before his death.

"I wish I had retained it and sold it instead," Rosenthal once said. "I'd have been able to buy everyone a drink at the Baseball Writers dinner in New York, and thrown in a lavish tip."

## RED PATTERSON

**Red Patterson was a publicity director for the Brooklyn Dodgers during their glory days in the late forties and early fifties. After a salary dispute, he moved across town to the Yankees. He was handling the press for the Bronx Bombers on April 17, 1953.**

---

"I was sitting in the press box just watching the game in Washington when Mantle came up for the first time against Chuck Stobbs, a journeyman left-hander with the Senators," Patterson wrote in a memoir. "I saw Mickey hit this medium speed fastball, maybe 85 miles an hour. The ball just rocketed off his bat like no ball I had ever seen before. It climbed high into the air. It cleared the left-field fence, grazed a scoreboard sign above the old Griffith Stadium, and continued on a rising arch into the street beyond. Everybody was screaming in the press box. I said, 'Whew, I've never seen anything like that.' I

*John McEnroe, a legend in his own right, calls Mick his idol.*
Photo courtesy of the Mantle family.

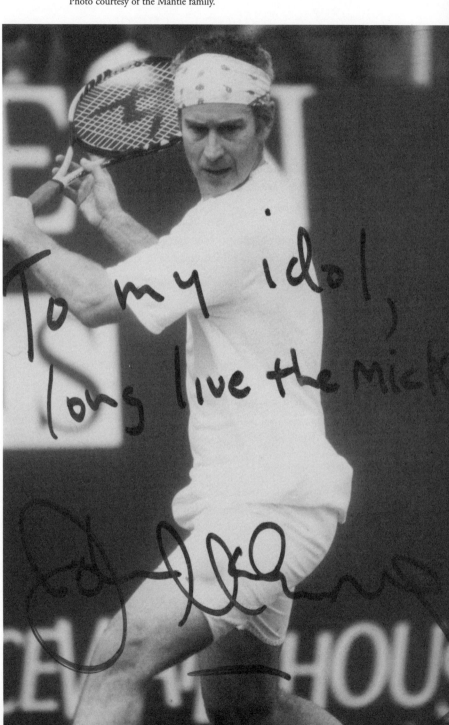

had seen a lot of balls fly out of Ebbets Field in right that went into the street or the garage beyond Bedford Avenue. Nothing this hard. I decided to give it an actual distance. I left the press box, walked down the ramp, bought myself a hot dog and a beer, stayed in the stands about 15 minutes, and came back to announce, 'The ball went 565 feet.' Who could challenge it? When I left the press box it was probably *still* rolling. Every single writer used that figure—565 feet. It became a famous number around Mantle's career. Even Chuck Stobbs, the pitcher, once thanked me for making up the number. He knew it made him famous."

## CLAIRE RUTH

**Claire Ruth, the widow of Babe Ruth, who basked in the warmth of her husband's fame for many years after Ruth's 1948 death, was a frequent visitor to Yankee Stadium during the 1961 home-run chase. Roger Maris and Mickey Mantle were after Babe's 1927 record of 60 homers.**

"Babe was very proud of that home-run record," she told sportswriters that summer of 1961. "I think he would have liked to hold on to it forever. But if it is to be broken I think Babe would be glad if it was broken by a Yankee."

As the home-run race heated up to a furious pitch in September, Maris pulled into the lead. He eventually hit homer number 61—on the last day of the season off Boston right-hander Tracy Stallard.

"I think Babe would have wanted Mickey to do it," Claire Ruth confessed in a later article. "He was the true Yankee, he was there the longest, he seemed like the leader on the team and just the right player to follow the Babe's lead. You know what? I gave Mickey one good piece of advice. I told him to get all the money he could from the Yankees. The Yankees were cheap with Babe, especially at the end. I think they were cheap with Mickey, too."

## STEVE PILCHEN

**Steve Pilchen is a fanatic Yankees backer from Iowa.**

———————————

Pilchen read in the papers one year that the Yankees had opened a fantasy camp and that Mickey Mantle would attend and work with the campers. The camp week cost $5,000. Pilchen, who worked as a social worker and moonlighted as a security guard, saved all his money for several months and made it to the camp.

Mantle took one look at the short, overweight Pilchen and kidded him.

"Hey, where did you get that gut? In a pillow store?" said Mantle.

"Nah, I just eat a lot," said Pilchen.

"You mean all the time," said Mickey.

"Ahh, it didn't hurt Babe Ruth being fat," Pilchen said.

"Yeah," said Mantle, "but he could play baseball."

## JOHN DREBINGER

**John Drebinger was a *New York Times* sportswriter for more than 40 years. He ended his working days as an assistant in the Yankees publicity office. He was still working when he died in his late nineties in 1976.**

———————————

"Mickey approached me once and asked if anybody had ever hit a fair ball out of Yankee Stadium," Drebinger told Maury Allen many years ago. "I told him there had been a rumor that Negro League star Josh Gibson had done it during the thirties. Nobody could prove it."

"Do you think anybody can do it?" Mantle asked Drebinger.

"I'll believe it when I see it," replied the *Times* man.

On May 22, 1963, he almost saw it.

The Yankees were playing the Kansas City A's. Mantle, batting left-handed, faced the Kansas City reliever Bill Fischer.

"I threw him a high fastball," said Fischer, a longtime pitching coach in the big leagues. "I thought maybe he would pop it up."

Mantle caught the ball at the perfect moment of his swing and drove the ball to the third deck of the old Yankee Stadium. It kept rising as it flew near the old facade of the Stadium where not even Babe Ruth cleared the top. At the last instant the ball touched the edge of the facade and bounced back hard on the field. It may have traveled more than 600 feet.

After the game, Maury Allen asked Mantle about the blast.

"I think I got all of it," he laughed.

"Is that your longest ever?" Allen continued, thinking back to the 565-foot shot off Chuck Stobbs in Washington.

"It had to be," said Mantle. "It hit the fuh-card."

It became standard New York language when any long fly ball went out that way to describe how close it came to hitting the "fuh-card" Mickey Mantle's pronunciation of the facing on that famous third deck.

After the blow, John Drebinger, a renowned big eater, came into the clubhouse and said, "Get me another sandwich. Now I've seen everything!"

## STEPHEN TAMBONE

**Stephen Tambone, a retired Dallas businessman, grew up in the Bronx. He waited all night outside of Lovers Lane United Methodist Church in Dallas when Mickey's funeral was held there in 1995.**

*Mick points to a scuff on the ball that he hit out of Griffith Stadium on April 17, 1953. The tape-measure shot hit a house across the street.* Photo courtesy of AP/Wide World Photos.

"I remembered him as a kid Yankee in the Stadium. The moment I saw him he became my favorite. There was just something so special about Mickey. We all dreamed we could be like him, handsome, impressive, and a huge home-run hitter. Ahh, there was only one Mickey. I used to go to almost every game in the Stadium in 1951 and 1952. I traveled here because I just wanted to say good-bye to my old friend."

## ROD CAREW

**Rod Carew was one of the finest hitters of his time. He was born in Panama and grew up in the Bronx, New York. He often played opposite Yankee Stadium in Macombs Dam Park. He was elected to the Hall of Fame in 1991.**

"I always liked Mickey Mantle. He was my favorite Yankee. I tried out with the Yankees as a kid and hit a lot of line drives. The Yankees wouldn't sign me. They wanted every kid to be another Mickey Mantle. They liked you if you showed you could hit balls into the stands. I guess you can say Mickey kept me from being a Yankee. Then I signed with the Twins. One day we were playing the Yankees and I hit a huge drive to center field. It went between the monuments and I got an inside-the-park homer. Elston Howard, the Yankee catcher, congratulated me the next time up. 'Hey, kid, you got some power. You might be another Mantle.' I couldn't stop laughing."

## GOOSE GOSSAGE

**Goose Gossage was the finest relief pitcher of his time. The hard-throwing right-hander retired future Hall of**

**Famer Carl Yastrzemski on a pop-up for the final out in the famous 1978 Boston–New York playoff game in Fenway Park.**

───────────

"My dad died before I made it to the big leagues in 1972. I got into my first game at Yankee Stadium and I had goose bumps all over. I just looked up in the sky and thanked my dad. Heck, this was where Babe Ruth and Mickey Mantle had played, and now I was out there. When I was a kid growing up in Colorado we always fought over who could be Mickey. We watched those Yankee games on Saturday as *Game of the Week*. Mickey always seemed to hit a homer."

## JUAN MARICHAL

**Juan Marichal was one of the smoothest pitchers of all time with an easy motion and incredible control of all of his pitches. Known as "the Dominican Dandy," Marichal won 243 games for the Giants.**

───────────

"In my country we used to gather around a portable radio in the streets and listen to the *Game of the Week*. We would be talking and cheering for the players, mostly the Yankees, except when Mickey came up. Then we would all get quiet. We just wanted to hear the sound of the baseball hitting the bat when Mickey was up."

## REGGIE JACKSON

**Reggie Jackson, known as "Mr. October" for his World Series heroics, including three consecutive homers in the sixth game of the 1977 Series for the Yankees against the**

**Dodgers, hit 563 home runs. He was elected to the Hall of Fame in 1993.**

———————————

"I was with the Kansas City A's after coming up from the minors in 1967. I ran off the field at the end of an inning in a game against the Yankees. I looked up and I was crossing paths with Mickey Mantle. He was running to first base. He looked at me and just said, 'Go ahead, Reggie.' He knew my name. It took my breath away. I couldn't say a thing. I just looked down and saw his shoes. They had the big No. 7 on them. I just got goose bumps all over my body."

When Reggie broke Mickey's career home-run record with his 537th home run in California, Mantle joined him on the field for the huge celebration.

With Reggie beaming at his side, Mickey said, "When you hit 536, 537 home runs like we did, and strike out as much as we did, you know you must be doing something right."

## PAT SUMMERALL

**Pat Summerall was the greatest kicker the New York football Giants ever had. He played for the Giants from 1958 through 1961. He then became an NFL broadcaster and teamed with John Madden as the best in the business for many years. He was one of Mickey Mantle's closest friends for nearly half a century.**

———————————

"I first met Mickey when I was playing minor league ball in Oklahoma and he was with the farm club in Joplin, Missouri, in 1949. We were about the same age, both scared kids out of the South and both trying to make it as pro athletes. I was having trouble with the curveball, and my manager came up to me one day and said, 'Hey, I hear you play a little football.' When I said I did, he said, 'I think that's the direction your athletic career should take.' That ended my baseball career but was just the start of the friendship. I played football for the St. Louis Cardinals and then came to the New York Giants in 1958. Mickey was already the greatest star in the game. I had seen him every time I was visiting in New York, and we would have dinner and hit a lot of those nightclubs together.

"It was very hard for Mickey because he was so popular and so well known. See, Mickey was like the first great rock star. He was bigger than Presley, bigger than the Beatles, bigger than all of them. People would just gang up on him and hardly let go. He couldn't go out in public without a big fuss being made of him. I was just the other guy and I tried to keep people away. It was pretty difficult.

"The one time we could have a good time together without anybody bothering us was when we played golf. We used to play golf together in Dallas all the time. After he quit playing baseball, we continued our golf games. Then people started waiting for him to come off the course. They would gather around him for autographs. One day he got a good idea. He went out and had some picture postcards made up and signed them. When people came up to him, he would give out the signed cards and that would get rid of a lot of them.

"We always had fun together. We had lots of laughs and enjoyed ourselves at night when we would lift a few. Every so often he would get in a down mood, get a little sad and say, 'I wish I wasn't Mickey Mantle.' He just meant the burden of being that famous, having so many people fuss over him. It could just get to be too much. He loved playing, he loved the game, he loved the competition. What he *didn't* love was all the fuss about being Mickey Mantle that went with it.

"Mickey wasn't feeling too good in his later years. I wasn't feeling too good myself. After all those years of holding up a lot of bar stools I went into the Betty Ford Clinic, and it really saved my life. I feel better than I ever felt before. One day

Life of a Legend, *captured in an oil painting by renowned artist Terry Fogarty.*

Mickey, who knew about my stay out there in California, looked at me and said, 'Do you have any fun out there?' I told him it wasn't for fun. It was for getting healthy. He finally went to Betty Ford, and I think that he was really happy about that. It was probably the smartest thing he did in his later life. He didn't have a lot of years after that, but he was healthy and sober until the cancer got him."

## DOMENIC SANDIFER

**Domenic Sandifer is a senior vice president at Universal Music Group, heading strategic marketing. A graduate of UCLA and a member of the Bruin football team, Sandifer's first job out of college was as director of athlete relations for the Upper Deck Company, which was, at that time, the world's largest sports memorabilia and collectibles company. One of his many duties in the position was to travel with some of the Upper Deck athletes to various promotions and appearances on behalf of the company. These athletes included Michael Jordan, Larry Bird, Joe Montana, and of course, Mickey Mantle.**

———————

"I guess I was only 22 years old when I was hired by Upper Deck and first met Mickey Mantle. Within the first week of my employment, the company flew me to Tampa/ St. Petersburg, Florida, to meet Mickey and oversee his participation in a huge local promotional event. My first real experience with Mick was an oddly surreal scene. On that day, our first together, Mickey and I ended up in the backseat of a baby blue, seventies El Dorado convertible cruising down the streets of St. Petersburg in a parade. Unbelievable!

"As our car crawled down the parade route, Mick waved to the crowd, naturally, easily, and with the confidence and assuredness only a beloved public figure could have. I, on the other hand, a nobody, formerly a face in that crowd, strangely found myself sitting atop the car and waving to the crowd—next to this living legend. The next thing I know the car has stopped and Mickey is now signing autographs for fans as they approach. Oddly, I'm signing autographs for those who for some reason think I'm somebody. And I suddenly stop and think, 'What the hell am I doing?' It was all so strange, so mad, but so real. Here I am, it's my first week on the job, I'm in a parade, and I'm sitting next to an American icon, one of the greatest baseball players ever to play the game, and I'm signing autographs. Yeah right! Nobody's ever going to believe this one. It's too good to be true. But it was true!

"After the parade, Mickey and I boarded a flight back to his hometown of Dallas. We were traveling first class of course. A skittish flyer, Mick downed a few cocktails and I tried to follow suit, not wanting to disappoint. We talked like fast friends, and then old pals. We talked about growing up and who our idols were. I remember Mickey asking me this question and swallowing hard, and thinking at the time that I was about to tell Mickey Mantle that my idols were somebody other than him. So funny in retrospect. I told him George Brett and Marcus Allen.

"'Yeah, I love that sommabitch Brett,' Mickey agreed. 'He's a hell of a hitter. I had him autograph a ball for me once, and I got it at home up on the mantle next to a ball Ted [Williams] gave me.'

"Then I asked Mick who *his* idols were.

"'Ted Williams and Stan Musial,' he responded immediately, and went on to regale me with stories of Stan the Man and the Splendid Splinter. Musial had been Mickey's hero growing up (the Cards' were the only games he could get on his radio), and Williams became number two after Mickey's playing days began. We swapped stories for hours and began to plan our next road trip, which would be to New York City. It was then that I told Mickey I had never been to New York, and you could just see his mind go to work on that little piece of info.

"'Sheeeet, Pard. You've never been to New York? Now that's my town. I have a room at the Regency, and you'll love my restaurant.' Mick seemed truly excited about my first trip to the Big Apple. I was excited that he was excited.

"The next day, Mickey called me at home—which once again took me back, because now I was getting calls at home from *the* Mickey Mantle. (I had to call my dad afterward to tell him who'd called.)

"'Domenic, this is Mickey,' he began. I was all ears. 'Give me your flight info for New York.' So I did, never even knowing or asking why.

"When I arrived in New York, I was a little nervous and disoriented. I figured I'd just grab a cab to the hotel, but instead I was greeted at the gate by a man holding a placard with my name on it. He said, 'Mickey Mantle sent me to pick you up, Mr. Sandifer.' He led me outside to the elegant stretch limo, and we made our way into the city. I saw the city skyline for the first time in a limo that Mickey Mantle had sent for me! Can you believe that?

"When we arrived at the hotel, to my surprise, we completely bypassed the front desk and rode up the elevator straight to my room. As I entered the suite, immediately there was a loud knock on the door of the adjoining room. I opened the door and in walked Mickey. His apartment was adjoining my room, and he'd set this up so we could open up the doors and just hang out between rooms. The other thing that I noticed that was rather hilarious but that he found totally normal and natural, was the sight of Mickey just walking around in a pair of the white 'sanitary' undershorts that the players of his day favored. Here was the Mick, hanging out in my room, in a T-shirt and shorts, barefoot, welcoming me to his New York home. Once again I had one of those 'I can't believe this is happening to me' moments. Not only was I standing in my hotel room with 'the Mick,' but he was treating me like we were old pals, smiling that country-boy smile and welcoming me into his world. It was one of those moments that I'll always hold in my heart and tell my grand-kids about.

"After a while, we decided to saunter a couple of blocks down from the Regency to the Post House Restaurant for dinner and a few cocktails. Nearly everyone we passed recognized the Mick and shouted various hellos and greetings: 'Hey, Mick,' 'Mick, you da man,' or 'Mick, you're the greatest.' And after we pass some people, we hear a guy say, 'Who's that other guy . . . is he anybody?' or 'I didn't know the Mick knew Donnie Osmond.' (I get mistaken for Donnie all the time.)

"I realized now for real that I was standing in the shadow of a legend as he walked on down the hallowed streets of New York, his playground, his pantheon. I could feel the history and nostalgia engulf me—and I was, for this instant, with him in his world. Pretty amazing stuff.

"After emerging from a dinner where the booth we occupied literally had a plaque with his name on it and was always reserved for him when he was in town, we continued the evening with a few more drinks at the Regency Hotel bar. As the laughs and good times continued, Mickey began to wear down—but not before one last surprising gesture. The man reached into his pocket, grabbed a wad of hundred dollar bills (I later found out he routinely carried a big roll of cash with him at all times), took my hand, and laid them on my palm and closed my fingers around the bills.

"'Kid,' he said, 'I want you to have fun on your first night out on my town.'

"'No, Mickey,' I replied, measuring my words, 'I work for you. I'm already getting paid for this. I can't take your money.'

"Mickey scowled at me and feigning anger and a slight sense of righteous indignation said, 'You better take the f***in' money. I want you to have a good time. And I'm gonna call you in the morning to make sure you did.' With that he got up from the table and walked to the elevator, heading back to his room. I watched him leave the room, all eyes on him, then on me, the strange companion of this New York legend, and I wondered at my ultimate good fortune to have made such a friend.

"So, having enjoyed the moment and not wanting the evening to stop, I did as I was told; I slipped the money into my pocket. It was way more than most 22-year-olds make in a week. I went off to meet some friends of mine who lived in the city, and to share this story with them. We spent the next several hours drinking and carousing like we were our own kind of Saturday night heroes, hitting some of the A-list watering holes around Manhattan along the way. The money and my new-found bravado seemed to give me an all-access pass to anyplace we wanted—we were kings. And the night turned to day.

"Sure enough, that next morning, Mickey came knocking on the door of the now-open passage between our two suites, dressed once again in his skivvies. He settled on a sofa across from my bed, tuned in to some country music on the radio, and proceeded to get all the details I could deliver about the night that was. He listened intently and laughed like hell as I told my first New York nightlife war story. He shared a few key anecdotes of his own from years past. We sat there and shot the shit for an hour or two like old college buddies before deciding to head off to Mantle's restaurant to start the day anew, and surely, most definitely, toward the creation of a few more tales good enough to tell the kids about someday.

"I spent a lot of time over the next several years working and traveling with Mickey. I've often said that he treated me like a son or grandson—his family made me feel this way too. The Mick was kind and thoughtful, funny and even sentimental—a simple guy, a good man. Sure he could sometimes be rude and impatient with overzealous or downright disrespectful fans, but he always treated me, and most people, with respect and dignity. I felt like he was a lifelong friend even though I only knew him for a short time. And I treasure the man I got to know—not the hero that everyone else idolized but the

*Mickey strikes a Ruthian pose during one of his playful moments in the Yankee dugout.* Photo courtesy of the New York Yankees.

simple man with the heart of gold. For whatever reason he
shared a piece of that heart with me. Thanks, Mick."


## TOM GREENWADE

**One of baseball's crimes is the failure to recognize the con-
tribution of its scouts. Baseball scouts are not eligible for
the Baseball Hall of Fame in Cooperstown. If they were,
Tom Greenwade would certainly have been inducted.**

---

"I started following Mickey when he was in high school in
Commerce. All you had to do was look at those shoulders and
see how he drove a ball from both sides of the plate. I went out
to see him on his graduation night from high school. Then he
was eligible to be signed. I knew how much Mickey and his
father wanted to sign and have Mickey play for the Yankees. I
offered them $400 a month, the going salary in those days, to
finish out the season at Independence, Kansas. Mickey's father,
Mutt, wanted more money, of course, and said Mickey could
make that much playing semipro baseball and working in the
mines. The Yankees said I could offer him a little money as a
bonus, and I figured they would go for eleven hundred dollars—
both the Yankees and the Mantles. That's how it worked. You
have to remember Mickey could hit but he wasn't all that big
and he was a terrible shortstop, real bad hands, awkward in the
field, and that arm that couldn't be controlled. Anyway, I told
him I would take the risk. You know how it is with scouts. If
enough kids you sign don't make it, pretty soon you are looking
for a new job. But I did love that swing and that power."

Mutt Mantle accepted the bonus and signed the contract
for his son, who would not be 18 years old until that October.
When Mantle developed into the greatest star of his time,
reporters often flocked to Greenwade's home in Kansas City
for interviews about the night he signed Mantle.

"I always told them he was the greatest prospect I ever saw," Greenwade said.

"It really wasn't so. I was always concerned about whether or not the Yankees could find a position for him. It was a good thing they moved him to the outfield."

## BILL "THE BAKER" STIMERS

**Bill "the Baker" Stimers is considered the greatest Yankees fan of them all. He is the unofficial Yankees historian. Owner George Steinbrenner gave him a free lifetime pass to Yankee Stadium after they met in 1974. Steinbrenner considered Bill the Baker—he got his nickname because he worked as a machine operator for the Entenmann's Bakery Company in New York—a good-luck charm.**

"I went to my first game at Yankee Stadium on August 30, 1952. I was five years old. My father, George, a Long Island Railroad trackman, took me to the game. It was Old Timers' Day. The Yankees were honoring their past managers. Joe McCarthy was there and Bob Shawkey and Bucky Harris and Johnny Neun, and, of course, the current manager Casey Stengel. Stengel had won the Series in his first year of managing in 1949 and won again in 1950 and 1951. He would win again in 1952 and 1953, five times in a row, the only time that had happened in baseball history. There were 11 players who were on all five teams, and they got that famous ring in 1954 for winning those five in a row. I think that's the most collectible item there is in sports. Anyway, you want to know about Mickey Mantle. Well, he was only in his second year with the Yankees, and he hit a home run that day. It went so far I could hardly believe it. I just jumped up out of my seat and started yelling for Mickey. He became my favorite Yankee that day and he is to this day.

"I started going to almost every game when I started working. I worked a day shift and could see every night game and every weekend game. I would miss maybe five or six games a year. Now I'm retired and I am at every Stadium game, day and night. If the Yankees are on the road I go to the Mets games, but I miss a few of theirs sometimes to stay home and watch the Yankee games on television. I saw Mickey coming out of the player's entrance after a game and he signed my autograph book. I was maybe 15 or 16 at the time, and he was rushing off across the street to get into his car. That's my favorite autograph. Of course, I have a lot more autographs of Mickey I got after he stopped playing. There was the one I got on September 23, 1970. Mickey was coaching at first base for the Yankees in those days. He would do half a game at first, and Elston Howard, the regular first-base coach, would do half a game. I don't think Mickey liked that. I think he felt it got in the way of Elston's regular job.

"I got one at the 1974 preseason Yankee dinner, and I got a few more when he was signing autographs on his books at Mickey Mantle's restaurant in the nineties. I got my last Mickey Mantle autograph at the Baseball Writers dinner in 1995 at the Sheraton Center Hotel in New York City. That was when the writers honored him along with Duke Snider and Willie Mays with the Willie, Mickey, and the Duke Award. That was some special night. That was the last time Mickey was in New York City. He got sick after that and died that summer, August 13, 1995.

"On May 28, 1974, I was coming out of the Stadium after a game and ran into George Steinbrenner. I asked for his autograph. We talked about the game. We had won that day. He said that I should come back tomorrow. He gave me a guest pass. A free ticket. I have been back almost every day since. My seat is on the press level right next to George's box. I look in there and see him and wave to him all the time. I also see his famous friends when they sit in his box, you know, people like Henry Kissinger and Donald Trump and all those guys.

"I think Mickey was the greatest Yankee. I cried on June 8, 1969, when they retired his uniform No. 7 in that big ceremony at Yankee Stadium and Mickey was introduced last, after Joe DiMaggio, I think for the only time. I go to Mickey Mantle's restaurant for dinner every night during the season when the Yankees are on the road and watch the game on the restaurant television. I don't think there will ever be another player like Mickey. Mickey was always nice to me, and I miss him around here on Old Timers' Day. August 13, 1995, what a sad day."

## DAN RATHER

**Dan Rather is the managing editor and anchor of the *CBS News* with a long, distinguished career in broadcast journalism going back to his youthful days as a reporter in Texas.**

"The time was 1951 and the place was Buff Stadium, home of the Texas League Houston Buffaloes. It was the end of spring training, and the storied New York Yankees were there to play an exhibition game before heading 'up North' (and at that time, all the major league teams *were* up North) for the regular season. That was enough to bring me and my father to the ballpark.

"There was something else, though, too: a much ballyhooed rookie outfielder from Oklahoma named Mickey Mantle.

"It's funny what you remember about the past. I recall that there was just a hint of salty breeze blowing in from the Gulf, mingling with the smell of freshly baked bread from the bakery across the street and the rich scent of thick, newly mowed grass on the field. And I also remember seeing something I had never seen before: a grounder took the shortstop deep into the hole and this new guy Mantle—who had taken off from first with the pitch—kept going around second as the shortstop made a desperate heave to get the runner at first. Safe at first. And by the time the first baseman got rid of the ball, Mantle was safe at third. First to third on an infield hit.

"My father, who fully appreciated the significance of this combination of heads-up play and hustle, turned to me with all the assurance only a father can muster and said, authoritatively, 'This kid is going to be the next DiMaggio.'

"Once again, father knew best."

## JANET ALLEN

**Janet Allen is the wife of coauthor Maury Allen. She worked as an assistant in the photography department of *Sports Illustrated* and later worked as a shipping company analyst.**

---

"I was with Maury on a trip to West Point in the early sixties. The Yankees were playing an exhibition game against the army baseball team, and the team invited the wives of the members of the press covering that game to go along for the ballgame and a later picnic dinner with the West Point team.

"After the game ended and before the players and the press came back to the team bus for the short ride to the picnic area, the wives of the sportswriters sat on the bus. I had a window seat and chatted with other wives while enjoying the beautiful scenery of West Point along the Hudson River.

"Soon a group of fans who had watched the game crowded around the bus. They saw the Yankees emblem on the side of the bus and moved closer for a look. 'Merlyn, Merlyn,' one fan yelled. There was a TV commercial running that year with Merlyn [Mickey's wife] packing Mickey's bag with a certain brand of soap. This fan thought I was Merlyn

Mantle. We did look a little alike since we were both blonde [author's note: and beautiful]. We both had short blonde hair, and we were only a few years apart in age. This fan pushed an autograph album through the open window of the bus. I immediately told him, 'I'm not Mrs. Mantle. I'm the wife of one of the sportswriters.' He insisted, 'No, I know it's you, Merlyn. Please, *please* sign this.' I looked over at the wives of the other sportswriters, who were listening to the conversation. They were laughing at the mistake. 'Please, Merlyn, please sign,' the fan continued. I could see he wasn't going to go away. 'Go ahead, Merlyn,' the wives on the bus said. 'Sign his book.' I took the book and in my most careful left-handed penmanship signed, 'Merlyn Mantle.' The fan could not have been more pleased.

"I told Maury the story on our way home. He insisted on telling Mickey about the autograph confusion the next day. Maury said Mickey laughed hysterically when he told him. Except for the very early years, Merlyn wasn't anywhere *near* New York, and when she was, it wasn't for more than a month or two. There may be some collector out there with an alleged Merlyn Mantle autograph. If he got it at West Point, he should definitely be worried about its true value."

*Mickey coming home at Ebbets Field after hitting what would be the game-winning home run to beat Brooklyn in the 1952 World Series.* Photo courtesy of AP/Wide World Photos.

SECTION IV

# Mantle as Ballplayer

## JIM KAAT

**Jim Kaat probably won more games than anybody in the history of baseball for bad teams. The Hall of Fame should wake up and put this guy in Cooperstown. He had 283 wins in 25 seasons for the Senators, Twins, White Sox, Phillies, Yankees, and Cardinals. He was a great fielder and a terrific hitter. He first faced Mickey in 1960 and was a regular starter against the Yankees in the 1961 home-run year of Mickey and Roger Maris. He has been a Yankees broadcaster for many years.**

---

"Mickey got me a few times and I got him. I might strike him out on a pitch and then the next time up he would hit the same pitch into the third deck at the Stadium. There were times when he would get me and I would just turn around to see if they could find the ball. I played a lot of years with Harmon Killebrew, and he could drive a ball as far as anybody. Mickey was a very special player and a great guy. He was a guy we all

141

looked up to in the game. Sometimes when he would hit one and you would see him jogging around the bases in pain from his leg, you couldn't figure out how he could do it.

"My first game was in Yankee Stadium. We used to warm up on the field near the dugout in those days. I looked over and saw Whitey Ford warming up to face us. I was with the Washington Senators then. I knew it would be tough. Then I saw Mickey Mantle walk over to talk to Whitey while he was warming up. Whitey didn't even concentrate on his warm-ups. I knew I was in trouble. I enjoyed facing Mickey. He was the best in my time. If he would hit one off me over the wall he would put his head down and run around the bases quickly. He didn't want to embarrass the pitcher. I always respected that about him.

"They used to let pitchers warm up right next to the dugouts in Yankee Stadium in the old days. I was with Washington then, and pitchers started throwing maybe 20 or 25 minutes before the game. This was 1960 and I looked over and I could see in the corner of the dugout, leaning on the bat rack, it was Mickey Mantle. I was pretty awestruck that he would bother to look at me. I think he got seven homers off me through the years. I remember this one time I threw him a slow curve that almost bounced in the dirt, and he went down and got it and hit it about 450 feet for a huge home run. When he swung, his bat hit the ground and I could see the dirt fly. I never saw that before or since. I always tried to get Mickey out on breaking balls and soft stuff. He usually swung over those pitches. He wasn't the toughest hitter for me. That was Al Kaline because he hit any pitch you threw up there and he hit it all over the field. But Mickey made you get excited on the mound when you faced him. You know, he caused the most adrenaline to flow, just because of who he was.

"I remember one time that year, 1960, and Washington was playing the Yankees at the Stadium, and Julio Becquer was our last hitter. Those were the days when fans were allowed on the field after the game. Bob Sheppard made the usual announcement that fans were supposed to wait until all the players had cleared the field before they could walk on the field and exit through those open center-field gates. Well, Becquer hits a long fly ball to center, and Mickey goes back to get it. As he catches it the fans start streaming onto the field. All of a sudden I look up and I see several thousand fans on the field, and they are all running in the same direction toward center field and toward Mickey. I never saw such a thing. Mickey grabs his hat and his glove and tucks them under his arm and starts running for the dugout about 400 feet away. He looked like the greatest football broken field runner, dashing and dodging among all those fans trying to touch him or steal his cap or stop him for an autograph. That was something. They told me later Mickey played football in high school and was a pretty good runner. I could see that."

## DUKE SNIDER

**Hall of Famer Duke Snider was the anchor of the great Brooklyn teams of the late forties and fifties. He played on into the early sixties and even had a turn with the Mets. He was always compared to Willie Mays and Mickey. He was the lone left-handed hitter in a Dodgers lineup of mostly right-handers.**

"The amazing thing about Mickey is that he was a switch-hitter, as good from one side as the other. What a thing that is. He never had to face those curveball pitchers making him look bad with those impossible low outside pitches to hit like I did. I remember all those World Series games with the Yankees, and it always seemed that Mickey would get the big hit that would beat us. He was also one hell of a center fielder when he played in the Stadium, and he could race the ball down and hide behind those monuments to make a great catch."

## DENNY MCLAIN

**With his 31 wins for the 1968 world champion Detroit Tigers, Denny McLain was the last big-league pitcher to win 30 or more games in one season. He was 131–91 in a 10-year career cut short by gambling allegations, racketeering charges, and drug rumors. He was serving time in prison at Westchester, New York, when he talked of Mickey Mantle.**

"I had the game locked up, 6–0, when Mickey came to bat for the last time in Detroit in 1968. That was my 29th win. I had a couple of more starts and I knew I would get 30 wins. I walked off the mound and in a stage whisper I told my catcher, Jim Price, that I would let Mickey hit one. Mickey heard it and he asked Jimmy if I was kidding. He said I wasn't. I threw one batting-practice speed and he took it. The next pitch was over the middle again, and he swung hard and fouled it back. He motioned that he wanted it a little higher. He got the pitch right where he wanted it and drove it into the right-field stands. He ran with his head down as he always did, and then when he came to third he looked up a little and winked at me. The next batter was Joe Pepitone. He held his hand up where he wanted it. I threw the next one right at his head."

## ERNIE BANKS

**Ernie Banks, Chicago Cubs Hall of Famer, hit 512 home runs in 19 seasons—the best player never to make it to the World Series. He played from 1953 through 1971.**

"Mickey Mantle. I just loved watching him play. Maybe it was in an All-Star Game or just on television or in an exhibition game somewhere. I just loved to watch that swing. Both sides of the plate, lefty and righty. What a hitter. Plus I loved to say his name, 'Mickey Mantle.'"

## DICK RADATZ

**Dick "the Monster" Radatz pitched in 381 games without a start for the Boston Red Sox, Cleveland, the Chicago Cubs, Detroit, and Montreal. He was 52–43 in his career with 122 saves. At 6'6" and 230 pounds, he was the most intimidating relief pitcher in baseball until his arm went bad.**

---

"I faced Mickey Mantle 63 times in my career. He was 1 for 63 against me. I struck him out 47 times. It was just power against power. I always seemed to have more. One time I struck him out twice in a relief role, something pretty hard to do. He walked off the field the second time and he was screaming, 'The monster, the monster, the guy's a monster.' He gave me that nickname. It helped my reputation. It made me more intimidating to the hitters. I thank Mickey for the nickname. It helped me make more money."

## DON ZIMMER

**Don Zimmer has more than 55 years in baseball, starting as a shortstop in the Brooklyn Dodgers organization in 1949. He has managed in San Diego, Boston (he was the Red Sox skipper when Bucky Dent hit the famous 1978 playoff homer against Mike Torrez), Texas, and Chicago with the Cubs. He joined the Yankees as a coach under Joe Torre in 1996. He resigned from the Yankees after the 2003 season.**

---

"I saw my first game in Yankee Stadium in 1947. My pal Jimmy Frey (later a big-league manager) and a bunch of us kids from Cincinnati were awarded a World Series trip after we won the American Legion title. We were up in the top of the Stadium, but we saw Joe DiMaggio hit a home run. What a thrill that was. By 1950 I was playing pro ball in the Dodger organization. I got to play a few spring-training games against Mickey. Then we met the Yankees in 1955. Mickey hit a home run, but we won the Series. I don't think I ever saw anybody hit a ball farther than Mickey could. Guys would just stand around during batting practice to watch him."

## JOAN HODGES

**Joan Hodges—widow of former Brooklyn first baseman Gil Hodges, who later became manager of the world champion New York Mets—always went to the Brooklyn-Yankee World Series games. She has lived in Brooklyn all her life.**

---

"Of course, my favorite year was 1955, when we finally won. Gil caught the last ground out on a throw from Pee Wee [Reese], and we were champions. That was so exciting. Then, of course, we won in 1969 with the Mets. Gil was a great player in Brooklyn and a great manager in New York. I still can't understand why he isn't in the Baseball Hall of Fame. Gil always enjoyed playing against Mickey Mantle. Gil always hit long home runs. Mickey did the same from both sides of the plate. Gil respected him for that."

*Mickey, here a highly touted 19-year-old rookie from Commerce, Oklahoma, poses for the cameras during spring training of 1951.* Photo courtesy of AP/Wide World Photos.

# RALPH BRANCA

**Ralph Branca pitched in the big leagues from 1944 through 1956 with two World Series appearances in 1947 and 1949. In 1947 he won 21 games as a 21-year-old for the Brooklyn Dodgers. He gave up "the Shot Heard 'Round the World," the Bobby Thomson homer that won the 1951 pennant for the New York Giants. In 1954 he was a teammate of Mickey Mantle's on the Yankees for a short while.**

---

"Mickey was just starting to come around as a great player the year I joined him on the Yankees. You could see he was learning the game. He swung so hard on every pitch. I knew it wouldn't be long before he became one of the best in the game. He had that Triple Crown year in 1956. I was a great admirer of Mickey's. I wish I could have been a teammate longer. I might have won a few more games."

# JOHNNY PODRES

**Johnny Podres may be the most beloved Brooklyn Dodger of all time, pitching the team to its only World Series victory in 1955 with a 2–0 triumph over the Yankees in the seventh game. He pitched 15 big-league seasons and won four Series games. He served as a big-league pitching coach for many years.**

---

"In that 1955 game I had a great change-up. I knew if I kept Mantle from hitting one out, I had a good chance to win. He had enormous power from the right side of the plate. I got a couple of fastballs by him, and then I got him on a change. He hit it a long way, but it was caught. I can't imagine what would have happened if he hit a couple out on me in that game. Nobody would know who the hell I am."

## RALPH KINER

**Ralph Kiner was the National League home-run leader for seven straight seasons, from 1946 through 1952. He hit 369 homers in 10 big-league seasons and played his final year of 1955 with the American League Cleveland Indians. He has been a broadcaster with the New York Mets for more than 40 years.**

———————————

"I played a few games against Mickey in my final season. I was having back trouble and I knew I was finished. I could see that this kid would be the next great home-run hitter. Hank Greenberg came over from Detroit to Pittsburgh in 1951. He told me about this rookie Mantle who could hit them out both ways. That's something. Mickey swung a lot like me from the right side. He could lift a low ball and drive it. After I started broadcasting in New York in 1962 we talked a lot at exhibition games about his hitting. I would stand around the batting cage and watch him swing. It was really powerful. Then I would hear a groan. I think Mickey was hurting a good part of his career."

## STAN MUSIAL

**Stan "the Man" Musial had a lifetime .331 average over 22 seasons (1941–1963) with seven league batting titles and 475 home runs. He was an executive with the St. Louis Cardinals for many years and was elected to baseball's Hall of Fame in 1969.**

———————————

"In my early days the press used to compare my marks with Ted Williams'. We started about the same time. Then toward the end of my career it was Mantle's numbers they would put out there. We played a few spring-training games against each other. I would just watch him swing that bat from both sides of the plate and damage those trees in Florida behind the fences."

## AL LOPEZ

**Al Lopez broke in with the Brooklyn Dodgers in 1928. The affable señor from Tampa, Florida, caught 1,918 games in 19 years. He managed the Cleveland Indians in 1954 and the Chicago White Sox in 1959 to American League pennants, beating his old Brooklyn skipper Casey Stengel both times. He was elected to baseball's Hall of Fame in 1977. At 95 years old he recalled his memories of Mickey Mantle.**

————————————

"Why, you couldn't beat the Yankees if you couldn't deal with Mantle. He was the heart and soul of that team, a great player on offense and defense. Sometimes he would be in a slump and then he would lay down a bunt for a base hit and you'd look up and the Yankees had five runs. We had that great pitching staff with the Indians in 1954—[Early] Wynn, [Mike] Garcia, [Bob] Lemon, [Bob] Feller, and those fellows in the bullpen, [Don] Mossi and [Ray] Narleski, and they could handle him most of the time. Then in 1959 we had great pitching again with Wynn and Bob Shaw, and that left-hander, Billy Pierce, he really gave Mickey trouble.

"I've seen a lot of great ones in my time, and I don't like to say who was the best. But Mickey was up there with them."

## MONTE IRVIN

**Monte Irvin played only eight years in the big leagues because of the color line. He batted .293 in 764 games starting in 1949 and played in two World Series for the Giants. He was elected to the Baseball Hall of Fame in 1973 and spent many years as a baseball executive.**

---

"In the 1951 Series after we beat Brooklyn, Mickey was playing in right with Joe DiMaggio. Joe was my hero as a kid growing up in New Jersey, out in center field. Buck [Willie Mays] hit a fly out there and Mickey started for it and then held up as Joe called him off the ball. Mickey fell down and you could see he was really hurt. As great a player as he was, I always thought how much more remarkable he might have been if he didn't get hurt. That's a big part of the game, staying healthy all the way. Not a lot of guys can do that. Unfortunately, Mickey couldn't."

## SANDY KOUFAX

**Sandy Koufax is considered the premier pitcher of his time. He won 165 games in 12 seasons, struck out 2,396 batters, and won four World Series games. The handsome lefty from Brooklyn, always brushing back his dark hair with his right hand, was elected to the Hall of Fame in 1972. He broke in with the Brooklyn Dodgers in 1955 at the age of 19 but did not see any action in that Series won by Brooklyn against the Yankees.**

---

"I walked into Yankee Stadium and it was like walking into the Grand Canyon. There was nothing like it in baseball—the size, the history, the mystique. Babe Ruth,

Lou Gehrig, Joe DiMaggio, and now Mantle was carrying the team. I watched him hit a couple out in batting practice. I couldn't believe it. Then I faced Mickey in the 1963 World Series. They said he liked a high pitch. I just kept going higher. I was able to keep him in the ballpark. That was quite a thrill for me."

## BOBBY THOMSON

**Bobby Thomson hit "the Shot Heard 'Round the World," the 1951 homer that won the pennant for the New York Giants. Known as the "Staten Island Scot" for his home borough after his birth in Glasgow, Scotland, Thomson hit .270 in a 15-year career.**

———————————

"I remember that 1951 Series because of the high of winning it over the Dodgers to get there. Mickey Mantle was a rookie and he was in right field, and Leo [Durocher] said we would have to defense him deep. The word was out that this kid had enormous power. Then he got hurt trying to avoid crashing into DiMaggio on that fly ball. That was sad to see. I remember playing some exhibitions against him and a few games in the American League at the end of my career. What a ballplayer. You don't see many like Mickey come along."

## BOB FELLER

**The greatest pitcher of his time, Bob Feller, known as "Rapid Robert," was the standard of pitching power. He pitched 18 years, won 266 games, and was elected to the Hall of Fame in 1962.**

———————————

*Mick is congratulated by third-base coach Frank Crosetti during Game 3 of the 1964 World Series after defeating Ken Boyer (No. 14) and the Cardinals with his record 16th career Series homer.* Photo courtesy of AP/Wide World Photos.

"I always had a strong feeling about Yankee Stadium. I loved the challenge of facing DiMaggio. I came back from the navy in 1946 and pitched a no-hitter there my first time out. That was something to remember.

"I could still throw pretty hard at the end, so I enjoyed challenging Mantle. He had incredible power, and you knew he wanted to hit everything over the roof. I just threw it hard and high and he didn't do much with it. Of course I was at the end and he was just starting. Later on it might have been a lot different."

## TIM McCARVER

**Tim McCarver caught in the big leagues from 1959 through 1980. He batted .271 over those 21 years and played in three World Series with the St. Louis Cardinals. He has been one of baseball's most astute broadcasters for more than two decades.**

---

"I remember the 1964 Series against the Yankees and the awesome presence of Mickey Mantle on the field, just being a couple feet away from him, just watching him hit. I remember those terrible grunts and groans as he swung the bat, the terrible pain he was in playing the game with those painful knees and bad legs.

"In the third game, he won it with that huge homer off our knuckleballer, Barney Schultz, and he hit a ton, to everywhere. I didn't know this at the time and I didn't find out until a year or two before Mickey died, but he called that home run; he actually did. He told all the players on the Yankee bench he was going to hit it out and just end the game.

"Mickey Mantle. Just awesome."

## JIM PALMER

**Jim Palmer was the leader of the great Baltimore pitching staff for many years. The handsome right-hander had eight 20-game seasons in his 19 years with the Orioles. He was elected to the Hall of Fame in 1990.**

---

"I was 19 years old when I got into my first game at Yankee Stadium. I came on in relief with nobody out and the bases loaded. The next three hitters were Roger Maris, Mickey Mantle, and Elston Howard. I didn't know whether to pitch to them or shake their hands. I struck them all out and got out of the inning. I just walked back to the bench and said to myself, 'I just struck out Mickey Mantle. I just struck out Mickey Mantle.' I had a lot of thrills in the game but that rates right up there."

## HARMON KILLEBREW

**Harmon Killebrew hit 573 home runs and was elected to the Hall of Fame in 1984. His nickname was "Killer" because he crushed baseballs.**

---

"I was playing the outfield one day and Mickey was up. He caught one of Pedro Ramos' pitches and drove it off the roof of the third deck in Yankee Stadium. The ball bounced back to center field, and our center fielder, Jim Lemon, caught it on a fly. He held the ball up in the air and showed it to the umpires. He wanted the umpires to call Mickey out. Everybody was laughing. A few innings later I hit a ball deep to center field. It bounced past the monuments and went into the stands. I was chugging in to second and the umpire held up his hands. He said it was a ground-rule double. I looked at him and out to center field and said, 'I think it ought to be a ground rule triple, at least.' The umpire said, 'Maybe for Mickey but not for you, the way you run.'"

## MARTY MARION

**Marty Marion was a great shortstop for the St. Louis Cardinals and St. Louis Browns for 13 seasons. Overlooked by the Baseball Hall of Fame, Marion was the standard of shortstop excellence in his time and led the Cardinals to three winning Series in four times in the October classic. He later became a manager for six seasons. Known as "Slats" Marion in his playing days, he was a constant figure in the Cardinals' new ballpark dining area at Busch Stadium as boss of the operation.**

"I saw Mickey for the first time in his rookie season of 1951. He was an incredible talent. There just wasn't anything he couldn't do better than anybody else. He could run like the wind, hit with power from both sides of the plate, catch everything hit to the outfield, bunt for a hit in a key spot, and throw out a runner trying to score. One of the sportswriters once asked me if there was anything I thought Mickey *couldn't* do. I told him, 'One thing he can't do is throw left-handed. When he goes in for that we'll have the perfect ballplayer.' Even without that I would have to say he *was* the perfect ballplayer."

## TED WILLIAMS

**Ted Williams hit .406 for the Boston Red Sox in 1941, the year Joe DiMaggio hit in 56 consecutive games. DiMaggio was named the MVP. Williams often said that when he**

walked down the street he wanted people to say, "There goes the game's greatest hitter."

---

In *Sports Illustrated*, Ron Fimrite, in his article about Mickey in 1985, captured Mickey's thoughts on Williams and on his own style as never before.

> *A friend of Mantle's mentioned the name of Ted Williams. Mickey replied, 'Greatest hitter I ever saw. I didn't see them all, of course, but to me he was the best.'*
>
> *'And not just a singles hitter,' said Bill Dougall of the Claridge Hotel and Casino in Atlantic City where Mickey was working at the time for a needed $100,000 a year, 'like some of these guys with the high averages now. He hit the long ball, Mick. Like you.'*
>
> *In answer to the friend's statement, he said, 'Like me? Why he wasn't like me at all. He was a real hitter. I mean, he'd take that short swing of his and hit everything. Yeah, he hit some so hard they went over the fence. But he was a real hitter. Me, I just got up there and swung for the roof every time and waited to see what would happen. No, not like me. He wasn't like me.'*

## JOE TORRE

Joe Torre has managed the Yankees since 1996, with four world championships. His brother, Frank Torre, played first base for the Milwaukee Braves from 1956 to 1960 and was on pennant-winning teams in 1957 and 1958. He underwent a heart transplant in 1996 while his brother Joe was managing the Yankees to his first World Series title.

---

"I grew up in Brooklyn as a New York Giants fan but, I knew all about Mickey Mantle, you can bet. My brother Frank played against him with the Braves in 1957 and 1958 in the World Series. I joined Milwaukee for a couple of games at the end of 1960, and then in spring training of 1961 I was trying to make the team. I was 20 years old. I was catching in a spring game at Bradenton, Florida, against the Yankees, and Mickey Mantle comes to bat. He was wearing one of those rubber jackets that players used to wear in those days to help them sweat. They don't let you wear them now because they say it cuts off the oxygen to your body and can cause some serious damage. Well, he just looked enormous. Mickey wasn't a giant of a man, maybe 5'11" or so, but he had those big shoulders and big arms and just seemed to dominate the field. I think it was more his standing by then as the greatest star in the game. I don't remember what he did at the plate, but I think I just held my breath the whole time he was up there. He didn't say anything and neither did I.

"Then later in the game I was facing Whitey Ford. I caught hold of one of his spring-training pitches and drove it high out to right-center field. Mickey was in center and gave it a little chase and then just stopped and watched it as it cleared the wall for a home run.

"Ten years later, in the winter of 1971, Mickey was retired by now and I had had my MVP season with the Cardinals and we both were at a banquet out there in St. Louis. We were seated side by side on the dais and I was pretty nervous about that. I kept thinking about what I could talk about with Mickey Mantle. We sit down and he just starts talking about that spring-training homer I hit off Whitey 10 years earlier—1961—and he remembered everything about it, where it went, what pitch it was, and how he had to chase it only a couple of feet before he could tell it was going way over the wall.

"The last time I saw Mickey was in 1993 when I was managing the Cardinals and he was in town for a charity promotion. I think he had already been sick and he was involved in promoting transplants and getting people to sign those cards. Before going on the field he sat in my manager's office in St. Louis to avoid the press, and he kidded around about some old games and old teammates. He signed a bunch of baseballs they were going to give away that day, and it turned out they were American League balls. That's what they brought in for the signings. You could see how much he missed playing when he rolled the balls around in his hand over and over before he signed them."

# INDEX

organist, Yankees, 76

owners, baseball, Yankees, 23, 43–45, 68, 72, 76, 89, 92, 93, 94, 95, 100, 104, 105, 135, 136

P

Palmer, Arnold, 89

Palmer, Jim, 155

Patterson, Arthur "Red," 115, 117, 119

Pepitone, Joe, 13, 19, 32–33, 34, 76–77, 144

Pesky, Johnny, 69

Philbin, Regis, 59, 98

Pierce, Billy, 150

Pietro, Randy, 59

Pignatano, Joe, 36, 38

Pilchen, Steve, 120

Piniella, Lou, 66

Pittsburgh Pirates, 149

Plimpton, George, 94

Podres, Johnny, 148–49

Polo Grounds, New York, NY, 94

Price, Jim, 144

*Pride of the Yankees, The* (film), 105

Q

Quayle, Dan, 48, 49, 50

R

Radatz, Dick, 145

Ramos, Pedro, 155

Randolph, Willie, 18–19

Rather, Dan, 137–38

Reagan, Ronald, 68

Reece, Gabrielle, 50–51

Reese, Harold "Pee Wee," 112, 113, 114, 146

Reynolds, Burt, 93

Richardson, Bobby, 3, 10–12, 63

Richman, Arthur, 72–73

Rizzuto, Phil, 16–17, 51, 66, 95, 108, 115

Robinson, Jackie, 112

Rosenthal, Harold, 115–17

Ross, Spencer, 64, 66

Ruth, Babe, 18, 24, 27, 72, 109, 110, 112, 119–20

Ruth, Claire, 119–20

Rydell, Bobby, 64

S

*Safe at Home* (film), 88

St. Louis Browns, 156

St. Louis Cardinals (baseball team), 4, 7, 129, 149, 153, 154, 156, 158, 159
St. Louis Cardinals (football team), 126
Sandifer, Domenic, 128–32, 134
Schultz, Barney, 4, 154
Schumer, Charles E., 111–12
scouts, Yankee, 28, 107, 134–35
Seattle Pilots, 107
Seaver, Tom, 99
Selig, Bud, 107
Selkirk, George, 24, 84
Selleck, Tom, 83–84
September 11, 2001, events of, 74
Shaw, Bob, 150
Shawkey, Bob, 135
Sheehy, Pete, 7, 83
Sheppard, Bob, xiii, 142–43
Showalter, Buck, 74, 76
Simms, Phil, 66
Skowron, Bill "Moose," 8, 9, 10, 35, 47, 63
Slaughter, Enos, 17
Snider, Duke, 73, 98, 103, 136, 143
Spahn, Warren, 36, 38
*Sports Illustrated*, 50, 94, 138, 157
sportswriters, 73, 94, 98, 105, 108, 110, 115–17, 120–21, 157
Stallard, Tracy, x
Stallone, Sylvester, 51
Steinbrenner, George, 23, 43–45, 51, 72, 92, 93, 95, 100, 104, 105, 135, 136
Stengel, Casey, vii, xi, 15, 17, 20, 23, 24, 28, 29, 30, 33, 36, 38, 39, 77–78, 109, 135, 150
Stengel, Edna, 77
Stevenson, Adlai, 77
Stimers, Bill "the Baker," 135–37
Stobbs, Chuck, 106, 117, 121
Stottlemyre, Mel, 7
*Strike Zone* (Bouton), 4
Sugar, Bert Randolph, 69
Summerall, Pat, 125–26, 128
Sutton, Don, 106–7
switch-hitters, 14, 102